P9-CSH-216

Private Lives of Garden Birds

Calvin Simonds

Rodale Press, Emmaus, Pennsylvania

Copyright © 1984 by the children of Calvin Simonds

All rights reserved. No part of this publication may be reproduced or transmitted in any form or by any means, electronic or mechanical, including photocopy, recording, or any information storage and retrieval system without the written permission of the publisher.

Printed in the United States of America on recycled paper containing a high percentage of de-inked fiber.

Cover design by Anita M. Groller
Book design by Anita Noble
Art direction by Karen A. Schell
Cover and interior illustrations by J. David Umberger

Portions of chapter 1 originally appeared in *Horticulture*.

Portions of chapter 3 originally appeared, in slightly different form, in *Blair & Ketchum's Country Journal*.

Library of Congress Cataloging in Publication Data

Simonds, Calvin.
    Private lives of garden birds.

    1. Birds—United States. 2. Garden fauna—United States. I. Title. II. Title: Garden birds.
QL682.S56   1984   598   83-21118
ISBN 0-87857-479-4 hardcover

    4   6   8   10   9   7   5   hardcover

To my two great ornithological mentors:
Lovell Thompson, who taught me to love
birds as a child, and Peter Marler, who taught
me to love them as an adult.

Contents

Acknowledgments

Any writer who popularizes science builds his work upon an immense structure erected by the painstaking labors of other people. We are fortunate, all of us, to live in an age of great ornithological achievements, a time when discoveries are being made daily about the most basic matters of bird life. To try to condense all these accomplishments into short, readable essays is a humbling experience.

In addition to my general debt to ornithological science, I owe a particular debt to specific scientists who were kind enough to read drafts of these materials and advise me. Don Kroodsma, W. J. Smith, Howard Kramer, Ellie Brown, Susan Smith, Cheryl Logan, Alan Kamil, Ken Yasukawa, and William Shields all helped out in this way. Although I usually took their advice, occasionally the amateur in me took hold and I stubbornly maintained some of my homegrown hunches in the face of their expert contrary opinion. Thus, if keen-eyed readers find anomalies in the text, the blame should be laid to the author, not to the generous experts who assisted me.

Introduction

North Dana, Massachusetts, July 18, 1983

No doubt about it, today will be the hottest day of the year. Until eleven o'clock this morning, I was out in the garden hand-weeding the late corn, but the heat has driven me back into the house. With no air stirring, the temperature must have been well over a hundred down there among the rows, next to the dark earth.

Banished from my garden, I have taken refuge behind my typewriter. But even here, the heat seeks me out. I have opened all the windows of my study, but no breeze filters through the screens. Out in my yard, the fronds of the elm hang limp and still. Beyond my parched lawn, heat waves shimmer on the black surface of the country road. No traffic stirs. The only sounds are the somnolent hum of insect life and the desultory song of a red-eyed vireo sung as he sorts methodically through the twigs of a distant oak, looking for caterpillars. "First-on-the-one-hand . . . then-on-the-other . . . but-on-the-third . . . next-on-the-fourth . . ." Initially a soothing sound, the song as it continues minute after minute, hour after hour, begins to seem relentless.

The task I have set myself this afternoon is to explain to you, my reader, why I want to write and why I hope you will want to read a book about the *Private Lives of Garden Birds,* but in the heat, everything has distracted me. At the moment, I am engaged in a staring contest with a mockingbird. The mocker is perched on a twig of a small hemlock tree, inches beyond the window screen. We regard each other through the screen. He is so close that I can see the membrane flick up and down over his eye as he blinks. I know from my ornithology textbooks that his eye is better than mine—better at color vision, better at seeing details. Clearly as I can see him, he sees me more clearly still.

I wonder what my visitor makes of me and my typewriter. He keeps moving his head, shifting my image on his retina so that every second a new and eager group of light-sensitive cells is put to work interpreting me. At first I sit still, fearing to scare him, but eventually I tire of the staring contest and begin to work again. So intent is the bird in his inspection that he doesn't flinch, even when I shift the carriage on my typewriter to begin to type.

I must write—and you must read—a book on the *Private Lives of Garden Birds* because together we are engaged in evolving a new way of interacting with nature. Who am I? I am a behavioral biologist turned natural historian. Originally I was trained to investigate organisms as one might investigate rocks. I studied their movements and reactions almost as if the animals were objects rather than living creatures. Very early in my career, however, I became an ethologist. Ethology is a specialty of behavioral science that looks at nature from the point of view of the organisms that live in it. The founder of ethology was a German biologist named Konrad Lorenz, whose favorite way of studying animals— believe it or not—was to form personal relationships with them. In his early years as a scientist, he would swim with ducks and he learned to perform their courtship and fighting rituals. He became "mother" to numerous flocks of goslings and "companion" to a band of small European crows called jackdaws. Lorenz was tireless and ingenious in finding ways to see the world as his animals saw it. In many ways, my training has made me like Lorenz. I have become a partisan of animals.

And who are you? I assume that you, my reader, are an organic gardener, at least in spirit and ambition if not in fact. You may have a hundred acres of legumes, grass, and clover under organic culture, or you may have a couple of tomato plants in your flower bed growing next to a few petunias and marigolds. Or then again, you may be a city apartment dweller buying your food from organic farmers and gardeners in your region and biding your time until you can have your own garden. How far along the path to becoming an organic gardener you have already traveled doesn't matter. What matters is that you have taken the crucial first step in your mind toward viewing nature as a partner in your life, not as an antagonist.

And what does my science have to do with your gardening? Well, lots, actually. The way agriculture is carried out in our country has a lot to do with how we view nature, and scientists are the people we entrust with the job of telling us how nature works. Modern American agribusinesses tend to view nature as raw material to be exploited for profit. Most modern American behavioral scientists tend to view the organisms with which we share the planet as biological machines to be manipulated for the satisfaction of human curiosity. Science and agriculture go hand in glove. If we are to have a new agriculture that treats nature as a partner to be respected and negotiated with, then we must also have a behavioral science that approaches other organisms as sentient, striving, individual beings. My goal is to introduce you to such a behavioral science.

"Ah," you will say, "he's mad! He talks to the animals, and if I read his silly book he'll have me talking to them as well." Well, partly yes, partly no. We have all had the experience of coming to know a pet so well that we feel we know its mind and it knows ours. The feeling comes about not because we can "talk" with our pets, but because we know so much about their lives and their histories that we can anticipate their every action. From this intimate knowledge, we develop a sense of what it's like to *be* that animal. By writing this book, I hope I can help you gain the same kind of intimate knowledge about some of the animals with which you share your yard or garden. I have chosen birds to write about because of all creatures, birds seem to live in our world most fearlessly and most prominently. Because many birds are bold creatures, it is possible to come to know a few of them closely as you (and they) go about your business in the garden. Knowing them intimately, you are bound to become entangled in their day-to-day lives. After you have read this book, a stroll in your backyard will be like a stroll onto the stage of a complex melodrama.

So, then, I should write and you should read a book about *Private Lives of Garden Birds,* because from my writing and your reading, we both will gain a better sense of what it's like to be a creature living in a world so much determined by human activities. The more we know about the birds in our gardens, the more we will empathize with them and with all our fellow creatures. It is hoped that we will approach nature with caution, respect, and feeling.

In the pages that follow, you will come to know, intimately, the lifeways of ten different birds. In selecting our subjects, I have tried in every case to pick birds who are already acquaintances. For every reader of this book, at least half the birds in the book are probably regular visitors to your garden, and the other half are close cousins to regular visitors. When you get done with the book I hope you will be thoroughly familiar with what it's like to be a member of one of these species. You will know what the bird eats, how it passes its time, how and why it sings, how it finds a mate, and how it raises its young. You will know how you fit into its world and what it expects a good gardener to provide in exchange for its services as an insect eater and garden beautifier.

As I remove the last page from my typewriter, I see that my mockingbird visitor has departed. He cannot have been gone very long because the branch on which he was perched gently sways, the only one to move at all in the muggy, still air of this hot summer afternoon. Around the other side of the house I can hear him scolding something: probably the cat, who likes to lurk under the mockingbird's arborvitae on hot summer days.

1
Mockingbirds
Virtuoso
Singers

About the only thing I missed when we moved from suburban Philadelphia to the rural wilds of central Massachusetts was the mockingbirds. Mockingbirds are robin-sized grey birds with flashing white wing patches; they inhabit all but the most northern states. In Pennsylvania I didn't even need to leave my desk to hear or see a mockingbird. Every year a particularly vigorous one would sing from the cornice above my office. Anytime I wanted, I could open my window and hear his song. It was a marvelous stream of sound, sort of a classical, ecological music — not too repetitive, not too cacophonic — music to write natural history articles to.

But even though these Pennsylvania mockingbirds sang a lot, they didn't quite live up to their reputation as mockers. In fact, they rarely mimicked other birds. Local bird watchers with very keen ears would occasionally point out a mockingbird "doing" a cardinal or a tufted titmouse, but the identifications always seemed fanciful to me, more the product of the imagination of the hearer than of the ingenuity of the singer. I could see why mockingbirds might be called "concerto birds" because of the way in which their song wove in and out of the symphonic background of the dawn chorus, but I couldn't really see why they should be called mockingbirds.

Still, mockers or not, they were wonderful singers and I hated to leave them behind. You can therefore imagine my delight when one fall, two or three years after I had moved to my farm in Massachusetts, I saw a mockingbird. I was sitting out on the back porch one mild fall afternoon, contemplating the frost-scarred wreckage that had been my organic garden and wishing that a Big Freeze would come and put it out of its misery. I saw the mockingbird fluttering among the dead cantaloupe vines. He was there only long enough to flash me his white wing patches, but even this brief appearance I accepted as a gift. According to the bird books, he shouldn't have been there at all. Indeed, after a few days I didn't really believe anymore that I had seen him. Philadelphia and central Massachusetts aren't very far apart. But at that time, they happened to be on the opposite sides of the northern boundary of the mockingbird's range—or so the bird books said.

The following spring, in defiance of the bird books, a mockingbird took possession of our television aerial and began to sing for hours at a time. It sang as beautifully as any city mockingbird and—wonder of wonders—it also *mocked*. How it did mock! One after another it incorporated little bits of the songs of other birds into its own repetitive format: phoebe-phoebe-phoebe-phoebe . . . . . cardinal-cardinal-cardinal-cardinal . . . . . robin-robin-robin . . . . . meadowlark-meadowlark-meadowlark . . . . . starling-starling-starling-starling-starling . . . . . Practically every sound made by our mockingbird was clearly identifiable as the sound of another species of bird. In fact, I used the mockingbird to teach my kids birdsong identification. The three of us would lie out on the lawn in the front yard, chewing on ends of timothy grass and listening to our mockingbird sing. After each little burst of song, we would call out the name of the species all together in a chorus. The children learned to identify dozens of birds' songs that way.

We hoped that our mockingbird would stay and raise young, but we were disappointed. One cold, rainy May day he packed up and left. The farm seemed uncommonly quiet without him. We worried that in some way we had failed to make him feel welcome. Perhaps we should have put dishes of berries out for him. Perhaps we had too many cats. Perhaps we paid too much attention to him. Perhaps he didn't like being watched and overheard by all of us.

All that summer long, as I worked about the garden, I kept my eyes peeled and my ears tuned for my mockingbird. I missed him terribly. I love a good mystery to mull about while I'm weeding my carrots, and the mockingbird and his song constitute one of the great mysteries of science. Why should a bird bother to make so many different kinds of sounds? According to scientists, the songs of birds are supposed to identify the singer as a member of a particular species so that females of that species may come and mate with him and males may come and fight with him. A mockingbird's song seemed so inefficient. Chickadees manage to say who they are with a simple two-note whistle. By comparison, a mockingbird sings for half an hour and still can't manage to get this basic information across. Or so it seemed.

We never saw our mockingbird again that summer. But fortunately for me, the mockingbird has two cousins, both of whom live in abundance around my farm. Both are shaped a bit like mockingbirds: they are sleek birds with long tails. The smaller of the two is the catbird, a bird who is fond of perching in the depths of lilac bushes and mewing like a cat. The larger is the thrasher, a reddish brown bird that is often seen fluttering along hedgerows by the roadside. Neither species mimics other birds much and neither bird sings a particularly attractive song. But both equal or even exceed the mockingbird in the variety of what they sing, and thus the mystery of their inefficient song is as deep as the mystery of the mockingbird's song. So even though my mockingbird was gone for the summer, there was lots for me to think about.

That summer a young scientist named Michael asked to use my pastures and woods for a study. Michael was curious about how brown thrashers were able to tell themselves apart from mockingbirds and catbirds. Since all three species lived closely together in several parts of the United States, and since they all sang extraordinarily variable songs, how was it that brown thrashers weren't in a constant state of confusion about whom they were listening to? Michael needed several locations to study the brown thrashers, and I lent him my farm to use as one such location. He and I saw quite a bit of each other that summer. Two or three times a week he stopped by with his tape recorder and microphone to record what my brown thrashers were singing.

The traditional scientific answer to Michael's question is that brown thrashers tell themselves from catbirds and mockingbirds by counting. It is not *what* the species say that tells them apart, it is *how* they say it. Whereas on the one hand, a mockingbird says everything several times and a catbird says everything only once, a thrasher says everything twice. Bird watchers trying to identify brown thrashers in the field are told to keep in mind the phrase "Call me .... call me .... two-times .... two-times!" as a mnemonic device.

What Michael expected to find was that brown thrashers repeated themselves exactly once. He recorded thousands of brown thrasher songs and made pictures of them on a voiceprint device. All winter long he studied these pictures in his laboratory, and by spring he had made two extraordinary discoveries. In less than an hour of singing, a brown thrasher was capable of making a thousand recognizably different sounds. Never before had such a degree of song variety been observed in a bird. Michael calculated that if brown thrashers had a repertoire of songs in their head, and sang from that repertoire—as so many birds are thought to—then that repertoire would have to contain at least fifteen hundred songs in order for the thrashers to sing as many different songs in an hour as Michael had observed. All this the thrashers seemingly accomplished with a brain smaller than half a walnut meat.

But Michael's most startling discovery had to do with "twoness" in brown thrasher songs. True, thrashers sometimes delivered their songs in the pattern "two-times

5

two-times" as they were supposed to. But they also said other things, such as "two-times-times-times," and "two-two-two-times," and "two-two-times-two." In fact, the different sounds that made up a brown thrasher's song might be repeated once or they might be repeated several times. Poor Michael wasn't much closer to discovering how brown thrashers told themselves apart from mocking-birds and catbirds. Not for many months was Michael to think of a solution to this problem.

With all this excitement about brown thrashers, I almost completely forgot about my mockingbird over the winter. Consequently, I was again surprised when, the following spring, he returned. The circumstances of his return were rather bizarre. One Saturday morning in April, I had a very vivid dream. I was sleeping late, the slanting light of the morning sun was splashed over the bed, and I was restless and hot. In the dream I heard an oriole singing. "That's nice," I said to myself. Then I heard a bobolink singing. "Wonderful," I said to myself drowsily. A barn swallow's "switchit" call floated in through the open windows. I dreamed of new-mown hay and young corn thrusting upward through warm black soil. But when I heard a tufted titmouse, I came awake with a start. Even in summer we didn't have tufted titmice at the farm. I sat up in bed and look around me, dazzled by the sunlight. The room was cold. Summer had not come. The fields were still grey-brown. Up the valley to the north a snow squall stalked across the hilltops. There could be no orioles or bobolinks. But how vivid the dream had been!

Then I heard the oriole. "Oriole . . . oriole . . . oriole," it said. I leaped out of bed and ran out to look where the sound was coming from. I should have known. Up on the aerial sat our mockingbird, in his accustomed spot. "Bobolink . . . bobolink . . . bobolink . . . bobolink," he declared.

This time our mockingbird found a mate. Together,

the pair established a nest in a small blue spruce near the front door. From this central point they took charge of the dooryard. First, they concentrated their attention on other birds, harassing robins, brown thrashers, and blue jays. Then they began to concern themselves with the farm animals. Whenever the dog crossed the dooryard, the mockingbirds dove on him. And once the young mockingbirds hatched out of the nest, the parents took to pestering the cats unmercifully.

These mockingbirds were the only birds I have ever seen make a coordinated attack upon a cat. The attack would develop as follows. A cat would be dozing peacefully on the warm stones of the gravel driveway. The two mockingbirds would scold it for a while from a limb of the crab apple tree, and then one of the pair would plunk himself down right in front of the cat. He would brazenly spread his white wing and tail patches and dance from foot to foot, creeping up until he was only inches from the cat's nose. All the while he would make loud "tchak!" noises and an occasional rattle. It was a remarkable performance. I knew that aggressive mockers sometimes danced with opponents, but I had never heard of a mocker dancing for a cat. The cat would endure the performance for a while, and then, grudgingly, heave itself into stalking position. The end of its tail would begin to twitch. The mockingbird would continue his dance until the cat was wound up tight as a spring, its tail lashing, every sense, every nerve, every muscle mobilized for its planned leap at the mockingbird in front of it. Just then the dancer's mate would alight deftly and silently behind the cat, tiptoe up behind it, and goose it. The cat would come violently unsprung, expending all its carefully mustered energy in one violent, uncoordinated, twisting leap after its assailant. Both of the mockingbirds would now retreat to the apple tree and resume their scolding.

The mockingbirds were ready to repeat their performance endlessly. The cat would be slower and

7

slower to take the bait each time, but finally its hunting instinct or its predator's pride would get the better of it. No cat worth its salt could resist the dancing bird fluttering so temptingly near its claws. Each time the cat would prepare its attack more grudgingly. Each time it would plan its spring more judiciously. And each time, just as its muscles were at their maximum tautness, just as the whole cat hummed with predatory fervor, the second mockingbird would sneak up and goose it. You have never seen predatory dignity shattered until you have seen a stalking cat goosed by a mockingbird. The cat would eventually slink away from the dooryard, its tail slashing back and forth, and hide up in the barn where the mockingbirds couldn't get at it. By the time the young mockingbirds fledged out, they had the dooryard to themselves. No dog or cat or blue jay or robin would dare enter it.

But just as the mockingbirds' other antics became more noticeable, our male bird stopped mocking. It wasn't just that he sang less. We had expected that. Many kinds of birds sing less when the pair has eggs or young in the nest. None of his song was mocking song. In just a few weeks the amount of mocking had diminished to nothing. The bird identification lessons were over for that season.

That spring Michael was around with his tape recorder again. He had been cutting up recordings of brown thrasher song, mockingbird song, and catbird song and splicing them back together in new ways. First, he created a series of brown thrasher songs in which every unit was cut in half; these he called "catbirdized" brown thrasher songs; then he created a series of brown thrasher songs in which every unit was doubled; these he called "mockingbirdized" brown thrasher songs. Then, as a double check, he took mockingbird songs and cut them in half, and catbird songs and doubled them; these he called, respectively "thrasherized" mockingbird and catbird songs.

Now Michael was touring central Massachusetts with a tape recorder, his artificial tapes, and a loudspeaker. He drove around looking for the kind of overgrown pasture-land that brown thrashers are particularly fond of. When he found a likely spot, he would stop and listen until he heard a thrasher singing. Then he'd hang his speaker from a tree, retreat fifty feet or so, and play the different tapes through the speaker to see which one the thrasher liked best. *Liked* is perhaps the wrong word to use; *disliked* might be better. Michael's criterion for a response from the brown thrasher was that the bird must approach the speaker. The closer it approached the speaker, the better score it got. The bird would get a particularly high score if it buzzed the speaker the way warring brown thrashers buzz each other in territorial contests.

It was a rough-and-ready technique, the kind of science you do early in a research project when you are trying to get the measure of your animal subject. Michael was startled when it worked! The brown thrashers usually came to his speakers more when he played the song that had the number properties of brown thrasher song. This was true even if the song was originally a catbird song. "Twoness," or at least something approximating twoness, seemed to be important to brown thrashers. Michael was overjoyed.

The third spring I not only had mockingbirds at my farm, the neighbors had mockingbirds as well. All day long the birds at the three farms would countersing. Our bird would sing vociferously for several minutes at a time, and then, having exhausted itself, fly down to the lawn to feed. And then we would hear, floating up on the breeze from down the valley, the challenge of the neighbor's mockingbird, and still more faintly against the wind, the answering challenge of the neighbor up the valley.

All this competition must have just about worn our mockingbird out. It certainly wore us out. Our mockingbird used to roost at night in the arborvitae just outside our bedroom window. Sometimes I would lie awake at night listening to the silence and feeling the warm wind flowing in through the windows, and I would hear the mockingbird from down the valley open up. Pretty soon I would hear my own mockingbird, thrashing about in the arborvitae as if he was sleeping badly. After a time, he would begin to make noises, sort of like he was talking in his sleep—little muted chirps, peeps, chatters, and more restless thrashing. And if his neighbor persisted, the mockingbird would pull himself together, heave himself out of bed, as it were, and fly to the top of the arborvitae, from which he would launch into full song. On an otherwise quiet night the din was sometimes shattering.

That fall we had territorial disputes among neighboring mockingbirds. Off and on we heard the loud "tchack!" call that mockingbirds make when something that they don't want there is in their territory. Sometimes we heard strings of "tchacks," "tchakakakakakak!" When one of the mockingbirds in our yard gave this call, other mockingbirds within hearing would answer immediately with the same call. One day I was brooding over my typewriter and noticed two mockingbirds facing each other a few feet apart at the far end of the lawn. Their tails and heads were held very erect and they were edging back and forth like two fighters looking for an opening. Every once in a while one of the two birds would open his wings slightly and show his white wing patches. Sometimes the two birds would flutter up in the air, only to land elsewhere and begin their sideways hopping again.

This sort of territorial battle in the fall is unusual for most birds, but it is the rule for mockingbirds. In most parts of their range, mockingbirds ride out the winter on their summer territory. To protect their food supply for their own use during the winter, they aggressively defend their territories during the fall against any bird that eats the same food as they do—including, of course, other mockingbirds. When two neighboring mockingbirds meet along their boundaries, they perform an elaborate dance composed of fluttering and sashaying movements. The location of such a dance is a sure indication of the location of a territorial boundary. What resource my mockingbird was protecting I can't imagine. The autumn olive bushes I planted were hardly big enough to feed him for a week, let alone an entire winter. In any case, by Thanksgiving my mockingbird had given up his defense and gone.

With all the countersinging that season, we'd had more mockingbird song than ever, but still the birds refrained from mocking. As a matter of fact, our mockingbird wasn't mocking any more than the city mockingbirds I had left two years before. It was as if, under the pressure of raising a family and competing with other mockingbirds in the neighborhood, he didn't have time for such frivolity. Farfetched as that interpretation may sound, it still seems right to me.

In a way, our mockingbird pioneer reminded us of ourselves. When we first came to the country from the city, we were full of organic this and organic that, of woodstoves, of ecology, and various other forms of noble abstinence. Local people were amazed at how well we talked, but they were also a bit skeptical. And they were right to be skeptical. After a few seasons of frozen pipes, blighted gardens, devastated tree plantings, and perilous financial circumstances, we learned to temper our idealism. We have pretty much the same beliefs now, but we don't advertise them so much. We concentrate on singing our own song and don't bother so much with the songs of others. To proclaim yourself a pioneer is one thing; to *be* one is quite another.

As for Michael, we haven't seen him for years. During that winter, he stopped by to tell me how his brown thrasher work had come out. His problem was how to resolve the conflict between his first summer's work and his second summer's work. In one summer he learned that

11

brown thrashers use "twoness" to tell themselves from catbirds and mockingbirds. In the other summer he learned that brown thrashers don't necessarily say things twice. The paradox really bothered him. What good is it for brown thrashers to be listening for twoness if twoness isn't what brown thrashers say? If a singing brown thrasher sometimes says things as often as a mockingbird, and sometimes as seldom as a catbird, how do brown thrashers tell their songs apart from those of catbirds and mockingbirds?

The only way we could resolve this paradox was to conclude that brown thrashers *average* when they want to decide if they are listening to a brown thrasher. Even though thrashers sometimes say things several times, *on the average* they say things just a bit less than twice. Could it be that each bird listens to his competitors and computes the average number of repetitions over several songs? It seemed unlikely, but no other conclusion fit Michael's results. And still the fundamental question remains unanswered: Why should these birds do so inefficiently and with such effort what most birds do so simply?

All that happened almost a decade ago. The autumn olive bushes still aren't big enough to keep the mockingbirds here all winter, but the mockers come back every spring long before the brown thrashers and the catbirds. Michael is out on the West Coast working for a computer firm. He has no time for birds right now, but sometime I guess he'll get back to it. Mysteries like that of the songs of the brown thrasher, catbird, and mockingbird can be set aside for a few years, but they never leave you. Until Michael comes back to solve them, I will tell the three birds apart by counting: the mockingbird says things several times, the catbird only once, and the brown thrashers says things twice . . . sometimes . . . sometimes . . . sometimes. . . .

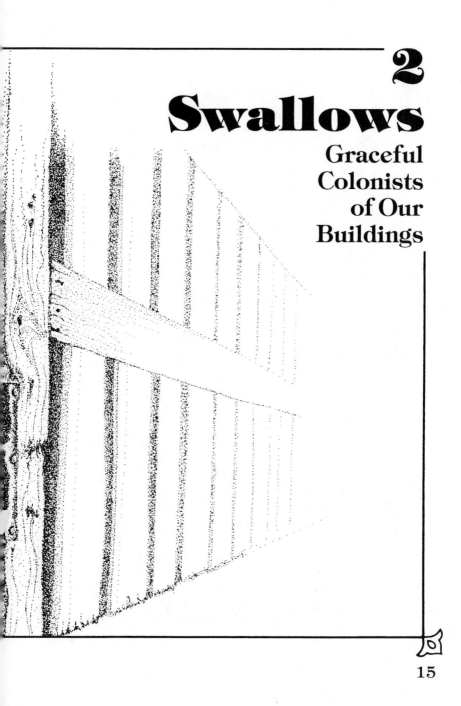

2

Swallows

**Graceful
Colonists
of Our
Buildings**

The behavior of the swallows tells me that I ought to be out in the garden harvesting. Instead, I am on the back porch dawdling over my breakfast: blueberries, shredded wheat, and milk. I keep extending the meal, adding first berries, then milk, then shredded wheat so that I have been eating desultorily out of this same bowl for the best part of a half hour. I ought to be out in the garden preparing for fall, but instead I am here on the porch savoring summer.

Swallows are everywhere. A pair of them hover a few feet from my elbow, complaining about my proximity to their nest. I am not sympathetic. Our picnic table was here before their nest. Down in the garden, other swallows are dive-bombing something that is hiding under the foliage of the pole beans—no doubt the cat is lurking there in hope of catching an unwary mouse or sparrow. Gusts of swallows swirl about the house and outbuildings. Against the sky swallows twist, turn, dive, and circle as they hunt for insects. As high in the sky as I look I can see swallows. It's hard to believe that in a day or so they will all be gone.

Watching the swallows play in the sky, I feel with keenness and a bit of dread the coming of the first frost. Before I planted my first garden and became involved with the day-to-day lives of so many living creatures, the coming of autumn would often catch me unaware. Throughout September I would be oblivious to the changes in the natural world around me. Then, suddenly, late some October afternoon, on a barren street corner under a grey spitting sky, among street trees as bare as telegraph poles, I would find myself wearing no hat, no overcoat, no gloves—and I would realize that summer was gone. Waiting for a traffic light to change, flapping my arms to stay warm in the wind, I would ask myself, "Where did summer go? How come we never have fall anymore?"

Now that I am a gardener, such insensitivity seems incredible to me. The tender plants that inhabit my garden have such trusting tropical souls. Working among them all summer long, I have come to know each as an individual. It is almost as if my nerves have grown out into their leaves. Sometime in early September my worst fears are realized. The cold air pours down the valley. The ridgelines emerge from the mist that has shrouded them all summer long, and the sun sets untarnished by clouds or by haze. As night comes on, the sky darkens, the stars come out bright and sparkling, and the temperature sinks. By morning the lush foliage of my tomatoes, peppers, beans, and melons has blackened in the icy air. Not notice the coming of *fall?!* I could no more fail to notice the coming of fall to my garden than I could fail to notice the sudden loss of several close friends.

So it is with a sort of wistful urgency that I linger over breakfast, watching the swallows. Frozen beans and corn I can buy at the market, but in just a few days the swallows will be gone for another eight months. They are irreplaceable. And so, in the end, I forget my harvesting. I stretch out on my back on the picnic bench and watch the hundreds of fluttering specks moving to and fro against the flouds. Even at this great height, I can tell the different kinds of swallows by the pattern of their flight and by the flashes of light and dark they make as they roll and turn in the sunlight.

If you gaze skyward from your own garden on a summer day, you may see as many as seven different kinds of swallows flying overhead. The first step in identifying them is to observe how they fly. About half the common species of swallows alternate between rapid bursts of flapping and short glides. If you spot a flapper-and-glider that flies in circles and looks noticeably darker than the other swallows, it is almost certainly a purple martin. Male "purple" martins are actually a deep royal blue over most of their bodies, and they are the only swallows that have uniformly dark underparts. Martins are colonial birds and can be induced to live in your garden in "martin houses." The traditional martin house looks like a miniature Victorian mansion set on a long pole. In each of the "rooms" of the mansion, a different pair of martins will raise its young. Because martin parents must catch tens of thousands of insects each day to feed their young, martins are good friends to have in the garden.

Another flapper-and-glider is the tree swallow. It, too, flies in circles, alternately losing altitude and then regaining it with three or four vigorous flaps. The adult tree swallow has an iridescent blue back and wings and immaculate white underparts. In nature the tree swallow nests in holes in trees, but it will also use nesting boxes. Gardeners who want to attract tree swallows place small nesting boxes on the tops of long poles beside their gardens, but tree swallows are not fussy and often are known to improvise. I have one gardening friend who had to give up his mailbox to a pair of nesting tree swallows one summer, and I know of many a gardener who put out boxes for bluebirds but got tree swallows instead.

Cliff swallows are flappers-and-gliders that fly an elliptical track in the sky. They glide downward for several moments and then terminate each glide with a sudden steep climb. Even though the flight pattern is similar to that of the tree swallow, the two birds can be differentiated by the color of their underparts. Seen from below, the cliff swallow is dingier, and if you look closely you can make out the patch of dark red under its throat. Seen close at hand from the side or from above, a cliff swallow reveals the pale rump and forehead that distinguishes it from all other swallows. Cliff swallows are colonial nesters and a colony of cliff swallow nests is a spectacular sight. Each nest looks like a hand-built pottery jug attached to the wall of the building with its slightly elongated neck pointed downward so that as the parent birds fly into the nest they fly upward. Cliff swallows make groups of nests on rocky outcroppings or on the sides of buildings. In the old days, when farmers' barns were not so well painted or were made of rougher wood, the cliff swallows were known as eaves swallows because of their habit of nesting under the eaves of barns.

The last of the flapping-and-gliding "swallows" is not actually a swallow at all but a very similar bird, the chimney swift. Although swifts alternate flaps and glides, their flight path is very direct. Unlike any of the true swallows, swifts fly in close formation. Here at the farm, groups of two or three chimney swifts zoom around the buildings all day long. They look for all the world like miniature flights of jet aircraft. As they fly, they twitter at each other continually as if they were conferring about which way to turn next. Swifts actually do nest in chimneys; if you have a chimney that is not used in the summer, you probably have swifts nesting in it. Watching them enter the chimney is a wonderful pastime. The little formation zips up to the chimney, stalls, and, fluttering vigorously, the birds let themselves down into the chimney one by one like a squadron of landing helicopters.

So far I have been describing swallows that flap and glide alternately as they fly. The other common swallows flap continuously and do not include regular glides in their flight. Among this group are bank swallows. Bank swallows flutter more than most swallows, so that their flight resembles that of a bat. The feathers of their backs and wings are a dusky brown and they have a distinct band across their white chests. Bank swallows are colonial. They excavate holes in steep riverbanks and sand pits. A sand pit that is home to a colony of bank swallows looks as if it had been used for artillery practice. Remarkable as it may seem, a bank swallow can excavate a hole one to two feet deep using only its beak, claws, and wings. The bird pecks loose the soil with its bill and then

19

thrusts the dirt backward out of the burrow with movements of its feet and wings. Both the male and the female work at the excavation, and it proceeds at a rate of about three or four inches a day. The digging could go faster, but, strangely enough, the swallows don't spend a lot of time at it. The excavation work proceeds at an easygoing pace and may take a week or more to complete.

The rough-winged swallow is similar to the bank swallow in many respects. Like the bank swallow, it is dark brown above and pale below. But unlike those of the bank swallow, this bird's underparts are dingy and the throat is a dirty brown. The flight of a rough-winged swallow is also different. This swallow flies directly and strongly without a trace of flutter, and it snaps its wings back smartly at the end of each stroke. The risk of confusion between the rough-winged and the bank swallows is made worse by the fact that the rough-wings frequently nest in the midst of bank swallow colonies. Lacking the bank swallows' skill at excavation, the rough-wings simply appropriate the burrow of some other bank-living creature: that of a kingfisher, or a bank swallow, or even the unused burrow of a small mammal. Fortunately for the rough-wings, both the kingfisher and the bank swallow often excavate more holes than they need, and the surplus is willingly turned over to the rough-wings for their use.

The last of the flapping swallows is the barn swallow. The barn swallow has many similarities to the other swallows. Like the cliff swallow, it has a distinctly red throat. Like the rough-wing, its flight is direct and strong and without a regular pattern of circles or glides. But unlike any other American swallow, the barn swallow has a "swallowtail," a deeply forked tail whose two branches extend one to two inches behind the bird. Seen up close, the barn swallow displays the most elegant of swallow plumages. Its tail and wings are a deep iridescent blue.

These contrast tastefully with the reddish brown throat and buff-colored underparts, which are a buff brown in males and a cream white in females.

Of all the swallows, the barn swallows are the most familiar since they nest under the roofs and eaves of our own dwellings. Since the behavior of barn swallows is similar in a great many respects to that of other swallows, to know a barn swallow well is to know a great deal about all swallows.

In prehistoric times barn swallows were cave swallows. They nested in the walls of caverns and in the deep overhangs of cliffs. Curiously, since taking up residence in human dwellings, the barn swallow has deserted its prehistoric nesting sites. Even though the same cliffs and caverns are still in existence, the swallows no longer use them. At my farm the swallows use each of the outbuildings of the farm, one pair of birds to an outbuilding. There is only one pair in the huge loft of the old hay barn, and there is only one pair in the tiny shed that is used as a workshop. The size of the building seems to make no difference.

I don't know why I don't have dozens more swallows nesting at my farm. Barns as large as mine have been known to support several dozen pairs. My father's barn, which is smaller, contains at least a dozen pairs, perhaps two dozen. Maybe the local food supply limits the number of swallows in my barn. My father's land is swampy and is one of the buggiest places in the world. My farm is located on the top of a glacial sandpile and is comparatively dry and bug-free. Perhaps my farm just doesn't have enough bugs to support a large population of barn swallows. Or perhaps the swallows don't like the entrance of my barn. My father's barn has huge doors that slide open. But swallows can get into my barn only through a small crack in the window. Perhaps the members of different bird pairs are not so friendly that they enjoy brushing by each other in the entrance hundreds of times a day. Whatever the reason, it's still a bit of a mystery to me.

The barn swallows I know best are those that share my garage with me. There is no doubt when they have arrived each spring. One day the garage is mine; the next day it belongs to the swallows. I come out in the morning to get into my car and am scolded for intruding on their garage. The pair swings round and round the garage giving their "switchit" call. After my swallows arrive, I park the car outside, unless the weather turns really foul. Four months a year seems a short time to give up a garage in return for the pleasure of having swallows.

Late as the swallows arrive each season, they still run risks of coming too soon. Because of its energetic flying habits, a swallow must feed constantly to keep itself alive. When the air is warm and the insects are abroad, flying and feeding present no problems. But when the air turns cold and dank or a late spring blizzard blankets the ground, then the insects don't fly and the swallows can get into serious difficulties. During cold spells they leave the dooryard and forage in large flocks over the neighbor's ponds, skimming insects off the surface of the water. If the cold weather holds, the swallows may retreat along their migration route or they may huddle in a corner of the barn in little groups, trying to conserve energy until the cold weather relents.

Late-spring cold snaps are a trial for swallows of all kinds. Bank swallows caught by a late-spring cold period will pack themselves into their burrows to wait out the weather. If the cold period is short, the swallows will survive in this way. But if the cold weather continues for long, the birds may die by the hundreds.

Once the spring weather has steadied and the birds are well fed, they bend to the task of rearing young. The first problem is to decide which pair of swallows is to have the choicest spot for nesting. For days the birds chatter and bicker and chase each other around the barn. These chases will often proceed with great vigor — around the house, in and out of the buildings, down across the lawn and suddenly high in the sky until finally the pursuing bird peels away and the chase is over.

The mate selection process in barn swallows seems to be a simple extension of this aggressive chasing behavior. When a male and a female swallow come to tolerate one another at the same nest site, then they are a pair, and will subsequently mate and raise young at that nest. Their courtship flight is almost indistinguishable from aggressive chases except that its outcome is different. The male chases the female, singing and calling constantly. Finally the female comes to rest on a perch near their nest site and the male flutters up beside her. She wiggles enticingly, the two touch bills or preen each other for a few moments. Then the male flutters up on her back and the mating is accomplished.

The mateship between a male and a female barn swallow is a fairly egalitarian relationship. The two mates participate about equally in building the nest. The female is the better builder of the two, however, since the male is often distracted from his building by the need to defend the female and the territory against intrusions by other birds. The nests are constructed on rafters or against the ceiling joists of barns and other outbuildings. If the nest is to be built on a vertical surface, the birds will choose a corner where two vertical surfaces come together or a place where there is some irregularity on the surface to give them a starting point. A knot in the lumber or a nail driven into a joist — almost anything can form the starting point for a barn swallow nest.

Both male and female work at gathering materials for the nest. After rain showers, barn swallows can be seen at the edge of mud puddles gathering up mud for the foundations of their nests. Swallows are said to use two

techniques for mud gathering. If the mud to be
transported is very wet, the birds carry it in their mouths
and squirt it out in little globs at the building site. If
somewhat drier material is to be used, the swallow rolls a
ball of mud on the top of its beak, carries it to the nest site,
and butts it against the nest. By these methods the mud
platform of the nest is built up of chunks or blobs of mud
cemented together.

As the nest is built up, it is more and more composed
of grass and other fibers. At first, the fibers are deftly
attached to the nest by gluing with mud. The bird arrives
with several strands of grass in its bill, presses them to the
nest, and extrudes a bit of mud from its mouth to hold
them in place.

When the nest cup has been completed, the swallows
will search diligently for soft material with which to line
the nest. If you have some feathers to loan them at this
time, you can see a delightful spectacle. Release some
handfuls of feathers into the wind, and the swallows will
dive and swoop for them like they were a highly prized
food. As individuals battle over possession of the feathers,
the feathers are released and grabbed repeatedly so that it
will be several minutes before all the feathers have been
gathered and carried off to the nests. Once lined, the nest
is ready for eggs. The whole nest building process usually
takes from one to two weeks.

The female barn swallow lays four or five eggs in the
nest. Incubation takes about two weeks. The female does
most of the incubation, but the male spells her frequently
so that she can feed. As with everything else a swallow
does, the exchange of mates at the nest is a deft and
graceful performance. The bird who wants to incubate
swoops into the barn, twittering loudly, and flies directly
at the tail of the bird incubating on the nest. At the instant
the relieving bird arrives at the nest, the relieved bird
takes flight and leaves the barn. The whole exchange is so

swift and so smooth that if you aren't watching it closely you are left with the impression that one bird has flown in and out of the barn while the other has sat calmly on the nest the whole time. At night the female always broods on the nest while the male sleeps perched nearby.

Even at this late stage the reproduction of the swallows can be brought to a halt by cold weather. If a sustained spell of cold, rainy weather occurs in late May or early June, the adult swallows desert the nest and feed for themselves over the lakes and rivers in the area. Without their parents to keep them warm, the eggs or young soon die of chilling. A few days later, when the weather improves, the adults return, throw out the little corpses, and start again. Often after a spell of bad weather in late spring I will find the floor of my garage littered with sad remnants of the swallows' failed first nesting attempt.

But if all goes well, in about two weeks the young hatch out and the parents begin to bring food to the nest. Nesting swallows are particularly useful to have around the garden because they consume large quantities of flies. The rate at which adult swallows feed their young is astounding. The two parents may make as many as fifty visits an hour to the nest and bring several flies at a single visit. Thus a single nest of swallows may account for the death of several thousand flies in a single day.

With all this food, the young swallows grow steadily. After about eight days they open their eyes, and in about three weeks they are ready to fly. When the young are ready to fly, the parents will no longer feed them in the nest. They hover near the nest and call excitedly while the young birds balance uncertainly on the edge of the nest. One by one, driven by hunger and restlessness, the nestlings finally take their first flight. Young swallows take a few days longer to fledge than many birds of the same size. The reason is clear: other birds have the luxury of being poor fliers when they are just fledged; swallows do not. As soon as they leave the nest, swallows are skilled fliers, capable of finding food for themselves. For a few days they seem to need the protection of their parents and perhaps a few tidbits from time to time to supplement what they catch for themselves. One often sees parent swallows feeding babies perched on wires. Sometimes they even feed their young in midair, the two birds fluttering together for an instant, bill to bill. For a few days the young return to roost in the nest at night, and family-sized groups are often seen flying together for a week or more after the young have fledged.

As you watch your swallows raise their families you will notice that they make a great variety of sounds. The two you will most commonly hear around the garden are the "switchit" call and the song. The switchit call is an alarm call the swallow delivers when it finds you in your garage gazing up at its nest or when the cat walks across the dooryard. An increase in the number of times you hear the switchit call in an average day tells you that the swallows have young in the nest. The more vigorous those cries, the closer the young are to fledging.

Barn swallow song you might not have recognized as such, because both males and females sing and because it sounds more like conversation than song. It is a long series of twitterings which the males punctuate with a burred, nasal, Bronx-cheer sort of a sound: "whichichachichachawhichichachichicha NYAAAAAAH ... whichichachicha . . ." Sometimes the song pauses there, but sometimes it continues with another series of twitterings. Unlike many songbirds who sing discrete songs, the barn swallow seems to be able to sing almost continuously.

Many of the swallows' other vocalizations have to do with courtship. The males give a call that sounds like a rising whistle when they are pursuing females in courtship. When swallows feel aggressive toward one another, as when a female is rejecting the approach of a courting male or when two males arrive to court the same female, then the aggressive swallow gives a chain of rattles or clicks known as the stutter call. If the female feels receptive to the approach, she gives a whining call and the male mounts immediately. Swallows also chirp a lot. The young chirp in the nest. A bird that has been captured chirps when it is released, and groups of swallows hunting together exchange chirps as they fly. The chirp calls vary widely from individual to individual, and their purpose seems to be to help individuals locate each other and stay together, either as pairs or in a flock.

By August all but the tardiest of young swallows have fledged out, and there is nothing for the swallow to do but feed and rest and wait for the migration. Since insects are plentiful, the birds spend long periods of time loafing on the telegraph wires and chattering to each other. Just before your swallows migrate you will notice a startling increase in the number of swallows around. For a week or so your skies will seem to be full of swallows. These are the migrants from more northerly places. Shortly after they arrive, they and all your local swallows depart. It's a sad moment in every year when the swallows leave. While one swallow doth not a summer make, no swallows doth surely a summer end.

As I watch the swallows eddy in the sky overhead on this late summer day, I feel an increasing apprehension. There is no doubt that having a garden puts me "in touch" with nature, but this being in touch with nature is a two-edged sword. I am glad that I sense the coming of spring long before my city friends. By the time they are boasting of their first crocus, I have already marked the return of the crows and blackbirds, heard the first song of the chickadees, and seen the position of the setting sun creep a quarter of a mile northward along the ridge of hills that forms our western horizon. But being in touch with nature also means that I sense the coming of fall long before my city friends. By June I have noticed that the mornings, ever so slightly, have begun to get shorter and by late June I have heard the chirring calls and seen the flocks of the first groups of fledging starlings. By late August I have seen the swallows preparing for their migration. They wheel and dive in the sky, they loaf in ranks of a hundred or more on the telephone wires. Only a few more days will I have them. I must savor their grace and good cheer.

3
Blue Jays
The Family Reunion at Your Feeder

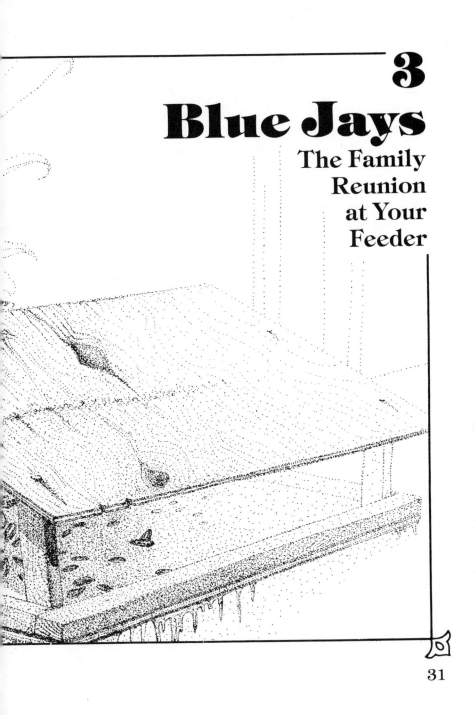

My neighbor up the hill and I have had an argument. She is anti-blue jay and I am pro-blue jay. This argument distresses us both, since we have seen eye to eye on so many other issues. I am in favor of organic gardening; so is she. She is against nuclear reactors; so am I. When the town votes to widen a road, we both vote No. When the town votes to establish recycling, we both vote Yes. But I'm afraid if we were asked to vote on whether or not to create the blue jay, we would definitely split our votes on this issue.

In fact, the blue jay may be the cause of our falling out. She said I *encourage* them. She said the word "encourage" with a kind of venom I thought would be reserved for somebody who kept rats as house pets or planted dandelions as a cover crop. She calls blue jays "bandits," and her feeders are of a specially constructed sort that are supposed to snap shut if anything heavier than a grosbeak treads on them. I scatter cracked corn and sunflower seed on the snow outside my study window in hopes that birds that don't object to my close scrutiny or the rattle of my typewriter will rummage through it. The blue jays are among the quickest of birds to accept the terms of this arrangement and so may be found flocked about my study window on any winter's day. So you see, I don't actually encourage the blue jays. I just don't *discourage* them.

My neighbor from up the hill said that blue jays are thieves and brigands just like crows. Technically, she was correct. The blue jay is a crow — or a member of the crow family, at any rate — along with ravens and magpies and some other birds of dubious reputation. To be a member of the crow family is to keep bad company, taxonomically speaking. In Australia and Scotland crows are said to pluck out the eyes of lambs, and herdsmen can show you enucleated carcasses to prove it. All over the world crows of various sorts are blamed for depredations of songbird nests. "Crested crow" is the translation of the Latin name given the blue jay by the artist-naturalist J. J. Audubon, and his drawing of jays shows them jovially dining on the eggs of a partridge.

But the blue jay's reputation as a nest robber is much overstated. Jays eat comparatively small amounts of animal matter of any sort, preferring nuts, seeds, and small fruits. In some parts of the United States they eat and store acorns, and in the old days they made good use of the chestnut groves that covered the eastern part of the country. Jays regard the eggs of songbirds more as a delicacy than as a staple. So even though I had to concede to the lady that the blue jay is like a crow, I didn't have to admit he was a thief.

"Nonsense!" said she. "Any fool can see that the blue jay is a thief because he wears a mask!" I told my neighbor that the next time she has a jay at her feeder she should look closely at its facial markings. They consist of three parts: an elaborate "moustache" over the beak; an irregular black line that frames the face, rather like a black scarf worn loosely about the shoulders; and a line that connects the scarf with the moustache through the eye. Each jay has its own distinct markings. The line through the eye may be thick and unbroken or faint with gaps in it. The moustache may be a delicate line across the bridge of the "nose" or it may be a heavy blotch that covers most of the jay's face. Usually the moustache has two or more prominent barbs that point upward on the forehead of the jay like worry lines, or downward from the corners of the mouth like frown lines.

To my eye, these facial markings give each blue jay a distinct expression. Last winter I set about trying to learn to recognize my jays as individuals by the expressions on their faces. I had seen a television program in which individual elephants were recognized by their ears; why not individual blue jays by their expressions? For a while this project seemed to go quite nicely. One jay who frequently came to my snowbank had particularly prominent frown lines at the corners of his mouth, so I called him "Sad." Another had very dark Worry lines between his eyes, so I called him "Grumpy." A third had very delicate, precise markings that gave him a carefree, youthful look, so I called him "Chipper." But one day I made a discouraging discovery. "Sad" was sad only when he faced to the right. When he faced to the left and I saw the other side of his face, he wasn't even glum. In fact, to my great distress, I discovered that "Sad" and "Chipper" were the same bird!

This unfortunate discovery underscores an important difference between blue jays and elephants. When you frighten an elephant, it turns and faces you and spreads its ears. You see all of the elephant's face and both of its ears. But when you startle a blue jay, it turns one side of its face to you. This is because birds and mammals "stare" at you in different ways. A mammal stares at you by examining you with both eyes and comparing the images it gets from its two eyes. A bird stares at you by looking at you with one eye and moving its head so that slightly different images are presented to that eye. It then compares these different successive images. The best time to identify an animal by its markings is when it is staring at you, because you have an opportunity to stare back. People who want to recognize an elephant by its face have to learn only one face. But people who want to recognize a blue jay by its "expression" have to learn two expressions. What is more, unlike the elephants, who stands still and gazes at you, the blue jay is constantly moving its head. Just as you get some detail of its facial markings in view, it shifts slightly and you have to refocus your eyes.

All in all, learning to recognize blue jays by their facial expressions proved to be too much for this organic gardener, but readers with quicker eyes, better eyesight,

and more patience might find the attempt more reward-
ing. And blue jays, who see each other up close day after
day, can surely use the facial markings—or "masks," as
my neighbor called them—to tell each other apart. Now,
even granting that the face markings on a blue jay look
like a mask, to call them a mask conveys the wrong
impression. Burglars wear masks to *hide* their identities.
But the mask of the blue jay *announces* his identity. So my
neighbor up the hill was surely wrong about the mask.
Would a bandit ever wear a mask that made it so easy to
identify him?

My neighbor also lamented that the blue jays come to
her feeder in greedy mobs. I had to object to the word
"mob." The society that convenes at her feeder is unlike
the society of any other familiar garden bird. In the
summer, blue jays lead a very ordinary life, one that any
robin or sparrow or thrush would be comfortable with. A
male and a female build a nest and raise a brood of young.
Parents share the responsibilities of parenthood. They
both build the nest and defend the area immediately
around their nest from predators and from intrusions by
other blue jays. The female lays the eggs and incubates
them. The male brings food to the female at the nest and
also guards the nest when she leaves to feed herself. The
eggs hatch in seventeen days, and the young fledge from
the nest about seventeen days later. Between hatching
and fledging, the young are fed by both parents. After the
young leave the nest, the family stays together for several
weeks. Even though the babies are as big as their parents,
they continue to panhandle food from them throughout
the summer.

In the fall the blue jay society begins a transforma-
tion. The young gather in great flocks and migrate south.
The adults linger in their area where they nested and
begin to form flocks with other birds from the neighborhood. This is no ordinary bird flock that wanders over the

35

countryside and whose members come and go as they please. Unlike flocks of blackbirds or robins, a fl⋯ of wintering blue jays is a residential community. It consists of individuals that have lived and nested in the area for many years. Its members have long-standing relationships. Some, of course, are mates, and the mated pairs associate particularly closely with each other during the winter. Mates can be distinguished from chance pairings of blue jays by the fact that they are willing to feed close together. If you see two jays peaceably feeding side by side, they probably are mates.

These blue jay groups have a very definite chain of command. As you watch blue jays feeding at your feeder, you will notice that they repeatedly displace each other. One will be feeding quietly and another will land beside it and the first will leave. Or the second bird will land and the first will move toward it a few inches and the second bird will retreat. These displacements are actually very subtle fights. If you know your blue jays well enough to recognize some individuals, then you will soon discover that some individuals are much more successful at winning these contests than are others. In fact, the entire group is organized in a sort of a pecking order—except they don't very often have to peck to prove it. The top birds are able to displace the middle birds, and the middle birds are able to displace the low birds, and so on down to the lowliest bird, who may not be able to displace anyone. These pecking orders are surprisingly constant and may even survive from year to year.

There is nothing casual about the grouping of birds at your feeder. The same birds come back, day after day, week after week. There is some absenteeism and some "dropping by," particularly during the fall and spring, but on most winter days you will find the same flock of blue jays attending your feeder. Year after year the same birds return to your feeder to ride out the winter. Even though your jays may hide out in the woods all summer long, when you get your birdseed out in the fall, many of the old familiar faces will return. Always there will be a few missing and always the missing individuals will have been replaced by some new faces. Often the new faces will consist of the children of members of previous winter groups who have mated and borne young somewhere in the neighborhood of your feeder. The children have spent one or more winters on their own and are now returning to their parents' flock to claim a place in it.

The blue jay's intense sociability has a lot to do with his evolutionary origins. Believe it or not, the blue jay is basically a tropical bird. I can just hear my northern readers exclaiming, "That's news to me!" But let me explain. The subgroup of "crows" to which the blue jays belong is called the New World Jays. Most New World Jays live in the tropics. The blue jays are probably pioneers extending the domain of the tropical New World Jays into some very untropical places like Maine and Minnesota. The interesting thing is that, sociable as the blue jays are, it appears that the tropical cousins of the blue jay are even more sociable still. We don't know very much about tropical jays, because they roam the canopy of tangled rain forests where scientists cannot follow them. What we do know suggests that their social life is more like that of monkeys or wolves than it is like that of birds we are used to.

Little as we know about most tropical jays, there is one that we do know about because it lives in the only part of the United States that is nearly tropical — Florida. The Florida scrub jay has an extraordinary social life that is carried on around its food source, the scrub oak. In the parts of Florida where these jays live, copses of scrub oak dot the landscape and each is owned by a social group of scrub jays. Each group of jays tightly controls access to the acorns that the oak trees produce. Either a jay is a member of the group and gets to eat its acorns, or it isn't and it doesn't! Among scrub jays there is no such thing as living casually at the edges of a group—either you're in or you're out. Because the food supply is so tightly controlled, breeding is controlled. Young birds who grow up don't automatically find territories and begin to breed as they do in so many species. On the contrary, each young jay must wait until one of the breeding adults in the copse dies and makes a place for it. The youngsters may wait quite a time because, like most jays, scrub jays often live several years after reaching breeding age. Denied the opportunity to raise their own young, the young jays pitch in and assist their parents in raising more brothers and sisters. An individual pair may have as many as six such helpers. And the helpers really do help. They attack predators, defend the copse against intruders, and even bring food to the babies in the nest. Nests with helpers fledge more babies than nests without, and parent birds with helpers live longer lives than parent birds without.

Once we know about their relatives, the scrub jays, the society of blue jays makes a lot more sense. Blue jays are "part-time" scrub jays. In the summertime the birds disperse locally, set up loose territories, and live pretty much like ordinary garden birds. In the winter, on the other hand, the jays organize themselves in a tight flock around a source of food. Probably before the settlers came to this country, that source of food was a grove of chestnuts. All they had to do to remain fat and happy was make sure they didn't share their larder with too many other jays. Nowadays, of course, the source of food is usually the feeder of some loyal bird watcher or organic gardener. Throughout the fall the blue jays take seeds from my feeder and tuck them away in places where they can readily find them when food becomes short in the winter.

All in all, I think "mob" is the wrong word to apply to blue jay groups. I think jays travel in troupes, rather like a

tribe of hunters and gatherers. My neighbor's jays are
actually sort of an extended family. They are parents and
children, grandfathers and grandmothers, uncles and
aunts, and distant cousins all gathered in from the
neighborhoods of the blue jay world to join in the feast.
The crowd at her feeder is no mob. It's not even a rabble.
It's more of a family reunion. But my neighbor is right that
jays are greedy. Nothing can empty a feeder faster than a
reunion of blue jays. Chickadees politely take one seed at
a time and eat it in sight of the feeder. Blue jays eat and
run. They cram their throats with seed and fly away with it.
And they return again and again until all the seed is gone.

Still, the blue jays' bad feeder manners have a good
side. One afternoon I watched the jays through a telescope
to try and figure out what they were doing with all that
seed. At first, they just flew to neighboring bushes where
they perched and ate, hawking the seeds up one by one
and pecking them with their beaks. But after a few trips,
they flew down to the ground and began hiding the seed
away. Sometimes they would just poke it into the ground
or into a crevice. On other occasions, they would go to the
trouble to put a leaf or other bit of debris over the place
where they had hidden it. I had often read in natural
history books that blue jays stored food, but I had never
imagined it like this. I had always envisioned a hollow in
some big old oak tree packed with sunflower seeds. But
jays don't store food as we would in a larder; they simply
scatter it about where they will be most likely to come on
it when they need it.

There are two ways that my neighbor up the hill and I
could look at this storage technique. She could point out
how wasteful the jay is, how it inevitably loses food that it
removes from the feeder tray and that might have been
there for other, more delicate species. But I prefer to think
of the blue jays as my food distributors. By feeding blue
jays in the fall, before the proper bird-feeding season gets

under way, I succeed in distributing birdseed all over the twenty or thirty acres around my house. Not only is the food available to the jays in the winter, it is also available to birds and small mammals willing to explore those same crevices and sunny slopes. The blue jay is the Saint Bernard of birds, carrying in his throat starvation rations for all the winter-beleaguered birds and small animals in my woods. And what doesn't get eaten goes to start the "volunteer" sunflowers that dot my garden.

This relationship between a blue jay's social life and his eating habits explains one of the great mysteries of blue jay life: why there are no blue jays where there are no people. Once, years ago, I wanted to record some blue jay calls in winter so that I might get really sharp recordings. I thought I would make my recordings on an isolated group of jays, far away from noise and disturbance of people. So I set out to walk along some disused railroad tracks, looking for groups of blue jays. In my part of the world there are many such railroad tracks that wander through miles of old pastureland, woods and scrub forest—just the sort of place you might think blue jays would like to be. But search though I might, I never found any blue jays out in the countryside. As I left town walking on the tracks, I would usually see jays perched near somebody's backyard feeder. Then I would walk for miles through the silent, empty countryside and see nothing. I wouldn't even hear any blue jay calls. But as soon as I approached another town along the track, I would begin to hear their calls and see their flashes of blue. It got so that I could tell I was approaching houses along the track by the sounds of jays down the track ahead of me. When I finished with this experiment, I had to conclude that human beings—and particularly, bird-loving human beings—are the life-saving resource that each group of blue jays depends on for its winter survival.

But the argument with my neighbor didn't stop there. As her final insult, she insisted that jays are noisy. Now here I really took issue with her. Noise is meaningless sound. The sounds of the jays are rich with meaning. Changes in the pitch and rate of the screeching calls tell me how excited the jays are. I know that if I hear the jays screeching loudly and rapidly I can look outside my window and see the cat lurking under the juniper next to their feeding ground. In the spring, a pair of blue jays often nests in the arborvitae just north of my bedroom. To be close to the jays is to hear all sorts of little private noises that most humans never hear. Mornings I can lie in bed and listen to the little squeaks and chutters made by the young and know just how recently they have been fed and how hungry they are. Sometimes the parents seem to hold conversations. They perch in the arborvitae and mumble at each other, as if they were reviewing the day's events.

And as for the blue jays' songs, nobody could fairly claim that these sounds are noisy. Their songs are known as bell calls. They are like short tunes played on a high-pitched musical instrument. A voiceprint of a blue jay bell call looks like a fragment of sheet music, with "notes" set out on a regular "staff." The calls are very quick little ditties, only a second or two long, and you have to listen very carefully to catch the tune. For instance, one of the songs around my farm is "doodeeleeoop." It is composed of four notes arranged low-high-low-high. Another call we hear often in the neighborhood sounds like "deedoodeedoo." This is the high-low-high-low song. I had to practice for a bit before I could catch the difference.

I told the lady up the hill that if only she would listen carefully to the songs, she would be in for a real treat. Soon she would start to notice that, wherever she went, she would hear different versions of the song. Each locality seems to have two or three of them, and neighboring localities share some, but not all the same songs. Pretty soon she could tell exactly what part of town she was in by the bell calls she was hearing.

Nobody really knows why jays should go to the trouble to have different songs in different neighborhoods, but I have a hunch the calls are like people's names. Each person has two or three names that identify him or her with other people. The last name identifies the person with all the members of the immediate family and with the members of the male line. The first and middle name usually ties him or her with the other family lines or with respected friends of the family. Like names, the songs that each jay uses probably tell something about its parentage and affiliations. Such an idea is really not so farfetched. Lots of young male birds learn their songs—at least initially—from their father and neighbors. Around my place in the summer we hear strange versions of the local blue jay songs, which we think are made by the juvenile birds as they strive to learn the local dialect.

Which song a blue jay sings may be very important to its future. In hard times the adult jays may use songs to decide whether or not to cooperate with each other. In this respect, these chaotic battles at my neighbor's feeder may be like family feuds in which individuals take sides and loudly announce their affiliations. It may be that only birds with a particular set of songs may gain access to my neighbor's feeder and that much of what she calls noise is actually the demanding and giving of passwords.

Knowing which song to sing may also help a blue jay get a mate. In the late winter and early spring, blue jays seem to have singing contests. The birds get together in excited groups and sing all the songs typical of their groups. Nobody is quite sure what all the excitement is all about.

One hypothesis is that the birds are picking mates. Just as male English sparrows take an interest when one of their peers is mating, the whole blue jay group may get involved in this mate selection of its members, perhaps because being mated to a group member means being accepted as a group member. Unless local groups of blue jays are to become dangerously inbred, they must from time to time accept mates from outside their group. It may be that all this bell calling helps the jays to establish the lineage or social "connections" of a potential mate of one of its members.

By the time my neighbor and I finished talking about blue jays, it was all we could do to speak civil farewells. It's funny how people can get so worked up arguing about a bird—as if winning the argument, one way or the other, might change the nature of the bird. I hope my neighbor and I can patch up our differences. I should hate to lose an ally on the recycling debate, and she needs my support on the issue of nuclear power plants. And as for the blue jay, we haven't been asked our opinion. Until we are asked, I suppose we might best talk about the questions on which we agree.

4
Chickadees
Faithful
Friends
in the
Garden

Today is the culmination of a month-long effort to train my chickadees to come to my hand. At first I wasn't trying to tame the chickadees—I was just trying to give them a bit of a break. A few years ago the chickadees joined the jays, sparrows, grosbeaks, juncos, and nuthatches that annually winter at my farm. Smallest birds of the lot, the chickadees seemed less wary of me than they were of the other birds. Unlike most of the flock, they never flew away in a panic when I opened the window to throw out the food. And as soon as I closed the window they would flutter down and start grabbing the sunflower seeds, long before the other birds could get up their courage. When the jays, juncos, sparrows, and grosbeaks returned, the chickadees would retreat and sit by impatiently, watching the other birds eat.

One of these impatiently waiting chickadees made an interesting discovery. He noticed that I often spilled a few sunflower seeds on the window ledge as I put the feed out on the snow. He taught the other chickadees to come to the window ledge to fetch my spillage. To reward their intelligence, I began to lay a line of seeds all along the ledge for the chickadees. This gift the friendly little birds accepted with enthusiasm. They would arrive to collect the seeds from one end of the window ledge, even before I had finished at the other end. So tame did they become that if I spilled seed on the *inside* windowsill, they would rap loudly with their beaks on the outside of the pane of glass, hoping to reach the seed. They sounded for all the world like they were knocking indignantly to get in.

When the chickadees came rapping at the window, they reminded me of a childhood neighbor I knew as the Chickadee Lady. The Chickadee Lady had earned her reputation in the neighborhood by hand-taming her chickadees. Whenever we children went to visit, she would put on an old army coat and a floppy old rain hat.

Then she would fill a cigar box that she kept handy with sunflower seed, and she was ready. She was hardly out the door, but the chickadees started to gather around. They perched on the brim of the floppy hat and on the shoulders of the army coat. They landed on the edge of the cigar box and rummaged eagerly in its depths for seed. They chickadee-ed and warbled at each other irritably as they struggled over who would have the best perches. It was as if my neighbor had charmed them.

As a child, I longed to be like the Chickadee Lady and have the birds come rushing to greet me when I came out the door. Several times I tried to imitate her. I got a cigar box full of seed and I stood by my father's feeder holding out the box. At first the chickadees seemed interested and gathered around to look at me, peeping at each other questioningly. But they never came to my cigar box to get food. If I stood still, they would come a bit closer, hopping from twig to twig. If I moved a trace, they would flutter away. I tried to stand very still, but my feel became cold and my hands stiff and my legs achy. Finally I had to conclude that I just wasn't the kind of person to charm chickadees. I emptied the contents of the cigar box into the feeder and returned disconsolately to the house.

I didn't learn the Chickadee Lady's secret until years later, when I was visiting my childhood home with my own children. We were out taking a walk and our path happened to take us near her house. As luck would have it, she was out in her garden filling her feeder. I waved and stopped to say hello, hoping that she might show off her tame chickadees to my children. After greetings and pleasantries, I made my request. She said that, no, sadly, her chickadees hadn't been tame for many years. My wide-eyed daughter asked how she had managed to tame the birds in the first place. "You must have been very patient," she said.

The Chickadee Lady looked at me and laughed. "Didn't I ever tell you?"

I shook my head.

"Oh, my goodness," she said. "After all these years." Then she turned to the children. "I have to confess to you that it wasn't me who tamed the chickadees, it was Annie. Wait right here and I'll introduce you to Annie." And she set off toward the house.

When she returned she brought with her the strangest contrivance. In one hand she carried what looked like a scarecrow. It was a crude, human-sized dummy made of grain sacks stuffed with hay. It was mounted on an old coat tree so that it stood up without support. The arms of the dummy consisted of two-by-twos braced out at an angle. Nailed to the end of one of these was a cigar box. The dummy's head was an old pillowcase stuffed with straw. On this was painted a smiling face, reminiscent of the face on a Raggedy Ann doll.

In her other hand, the Chickadee Lady carried the army coat and the floppy hat. She set the dummy on the law, slung the coat around its shoulders, pulled the hat down over its head and said, "This is Annie! She's the most patient tamer of chickadees you could care to meet! You just set Annie out on the lawn for a few weeks and keep her cigar box full. When you want to feed the chickadees yourself, you borrow Annie's coat and hat, fill your own cigar box, and go stand outside. In a few minutes you'll have chickadees all over you!"

So, last week when the chickadees starting rapping on my windows, I decided it was time to modify the Chickadee Lady's technique to my own conditions. I found an old leather glove that the dog hadn't completely chewed and set it out on the windowsill. Every day since then I have filled the palm of the glove with sunflower seeds. All week long the chickadees have been feeding out of that glove. Now I am going to see if I can get them to eat out of my hand. I open the window partway, and, without moving the glove, slip my hand into it. With the other hand I scatter sunflower seed in the palm of the glove. Now I await my first customer. Waiting, with my arm in the cold air, I have time to think about chickadees.

Chickadees belong to a worldwide group of birds known as titmice. Among titmice, tameness runs in the family. All over the world, titmice are known for being little birds who are unafraid of people and who take readily to feeders. When an English gardener fills his feeder, it is the great tit, the coal tit, the willow tit, and the blue tit who gather round to pick up the seed. All of these British titmice sound a lot like American chickadees, and some of them say "chickadee" without a trace of a British accent. Many are dead ringers for our own chickadees, complete with black cap and bib. Others are more colorful in their plumage, sporting a bit of green or blue or yellow in their body feathers, or a blue cap on their heads instead of the traditional black. Because of their colorful feathers, a British feeder covered with titmice looks a bit like a Christmas tree covered with ornaments.

The British titmice have carried friendliness just a bit further than our own chickadees have. They have learned to share the British gardener's breakfast cream with him. In England milk is distributed from door to door in small, bulky electric trucks, which because of their quietly purring ride and bouncy springs are known as "milk floats." At least until recently, milk was placed on customers' doorsteps in bottles covered with a foil cap. Decades ago an ingenious coal tit was investigating one of these caps. Attracted, no doubt, by its shiny surface, he was further intrigued by the hollow sound the foil made as he trod upon it. Since titmice, like our chickadees, look for grubs under the loose bark of trees, the feeling of something hollow under their feet interests them. Perhaps

49

the coal tit also saw his reflection in the shiny surface and thought he was being challenged for possession of his new toy by another coal tit.

Whatever the reason, this enterprising bird lifted up his tiny head and hammered at the shiny surface of the foil with his beak. To his great surprise, instead of piercing a white grub or grasping a mouthful of titmouse face feathers, he came up with a mouthful of sweet, heavy cream. What a discovery that must have been for a shivering titmouse on a raw winter morning! How smug he must have felt as he luxuriated in fresh, rich cream, while the other titmice in his flock picked over damp leavings at the feeders.

It is said that imitation is the sincerest form of flattery. If so, this particular pioneering titmouse must have been the most flattered titmouse in the history of birds. The habit of piercing milk bottle caps to get at the cream spread rapidly all over the British Isles. When I last visited Britain, almost nowhere were a gardener's milk bottles safe from his titmice. Every gardener knew that when he put out his empty milk bottles at night he must also put out a cover for the full bottles that the driver would leave in the morning. Unless, of course, he was willing to share his "top-of-milk" with the titmice.

Across most of the eastern United States there are two kinds of chickadees: the black-capped and the Carolina. Together they divide up most of the countryside between them; the black-capped occupying the North, the Carolina the South. The differences between the two birds are subtle. The black-capped has a bit more white in his wings and a bit more buffy color in the grey fuzz around the edges of his tummy. But so similar are the two birds that they have difficulty telling each other apart. In the Middle Atlantic states, where the ranges of the two species meet, they occasionally mate together. The most reliable way for humans to distinguish them is by their songs. The black-capped chickadee sings a simple two-note whistle, "Fee bee!" The Carolina sings four notes, "Fee bee fee bay." Otherwise, the birds are entirely similar in their looks and in their behavior.

Nothing about the lifeways of the chickadees appears to explain their extraordinary tameness, except perhaps their habit of forming small residential flocks in the same spot, year after year. The chickadees who appear so loyally at your feeder every winter form a flock that stays together all winter and defends your feeder against all other chickadees. Perhaps the members of such flocks are tamer than most birds because they have a better chance to get to know the peculiarities of the gardeners with whom they share their winter habitat.

Your wintering flock of chickadees defends a territory extending more than a dozen acres around your feeder. As the little flock travels about, it not only forages but it patrols the boundaries of the territory. The flock members keep in touch with each other with a variety of calls, among them a short, high-pitched sibilant whistle that sounds like "tseet!" and the familiar "chickadee" call. The chickadee call actually consists of two parts: a series of very short, high-pitched notes that sound like "pitterpitter" and several lower nasal notes, which do sound like "dee dee dee." The birds can use the two parts of the chickadee call separately or in conjunction with other sounds. Sometimes you hear sounds like "tseet-dee-dee-dee" or "pitterpitter-tseet" as the birds arrange the sounds in different combinations. The chickadee call seems particularly useful in helping the birds stay together, since each bird tends to utter it as he lands on a new perch. Thus, if a flock member hears the chickadee calls of his fellows drifting away, he knows he is in danger of being left behind.

The group of chickadees at your feeder is a well-ordered little society. Some of the group members are more friendly with one another than are others. These individuals can often be seen foraging near each other. Sometimes these friendly individuals are mated pairs, but sometimes they are just chums, friends of the same sex who get on well together. Chickadee groups are strictly organized in a dominance hierarchy. One mated pair usually dominates the other members of the group. The male of the pair dominates all the males and the female all the females.

If you watch closely the chickadees at your feeder, you can see evidence of these dominance relationships. Unlike sparrows or grosbeaks, which often crowd together to get food, chickadees keep their distance from one another. Although they look peaceable enough, the distance is maintained by subtle threats exchanged between the birds. The dominant bird will slightly fluff out the feathers of his black cap, and just at that minute, the subordinate bird will move away. If just fluffing his cap doesn't do the job, the dominant bird may fluff himself out entirely like a little puffball or he may lean toward the subordinate, open up his beak, and give a short two-syllable call that is the chickadee equivalent of a growl. The subordinate may then fly off, though if he is intimidated but wants to stay put, he may give a high-pitched peeping call, and lean away from the dominant bird. As a last resort, the subordinate will sometimes quiver its wings like a baby soliciting feeding. This imitation seems to deter the dominant bird from further attack.

Although chickadees winter in flocks, they breed in isolated pairs. The first sign that your chickadees are thinking about breeding is the "feebee" song. You can hear this feebee song on any mild, sunny day in winter, even in December. A chickadee singing a feebee song is not in a friendly frame of mind. The message in the song seems to be something like, "I'm a chickadee and I claim this territory. If any other chickadees think that they have rights over this territory, they'd better get their tail feathers over here so we can settle this thing once and for all right now!"

In early spring the mated pairs of the winter group divide up the winter territory between them. Since the pair territories are only about half as large as the winter territory of the group, and the competition for them is vigorous, some of the pairs lose out. The dominant pair of the winter flock gets first choice of the summer territories, and the best territory is likely to be the one that includes your feeder. Consequently, if you have a pair of summering chickadees around your garden, they are likely to be members of your winter flock and most likely the dominant members of that flock.

A male and a female own the territory together, and they share the work of defending it. You can tell when two chickadees disagree about the location of a territory boundary because you will hear their feebee songs alternating back and forth. If the disagreement is serious, the two birds will approach one another. When they can't settle the dispute by singing, they will face off on nearby branches, twisting and turning on their perches and making little high-pitched sounds. One bird may harass the other by repeatedly flying to its perch and replacing it, a maneuver that is called surplanting. If the fight gets particularly vigorous, all four pair members may get involved. Most often the fights are among males, but sometimes one of the males becomes so excited he attacks his opponent's female. From time to time a male combatant may break off the battle and seek out his own female nearby. It's as if he wants to make sure she's still standing by him.

After several minutes of skirmishing, one or both pairs retreats toward the center of their own territories. If only one pair retreats, it has lost the battle. The other pair will probably claim part of its territory. If both retreat, the boundary is likely to stay where it was before the squabble. As the pairs separate, they do so with scolding "dee-dee-dee" calls flung back over their shoulders, and even with occasional bouts of song.

By April the chickadees are sorted out into their pair territories and breeding begins in earnest. Chickadees have solved the problem of a safe nesting location in a unique way. Although they don't have a heavy beak for hammering wood like a woodpecker, or an aggressive temperament for stealing other birds' holes like a wren, still they manage to be hole nesters. They do this by excavating holes in rotted trees. They are particularly fond of birch snags, because the papery bark of the birch is easy to pierce but holds the tree together long after the wood inside has become pulpy and easy to excavate.

To the sharp-eyed observer, the pair gives away its nest site by leaving little piles of wood under the perches where the birds alight after a session of digging at the nest hole. If you find a tiny pile of wood chips in the woods, look in the trunks of rotted trees nearby for a small round hole. The nest hole will be no lower than waist height and no higher than about twenty feet. It may sometimes be in the rotten end of a branch that has broken off the main trunk.

About the time they are constructing their nest, the chickadees mate. As in many birds, the female solicits mating by behaving like a fledgling. She lowers her body near her perch and quivers her wings frantically, making a high-pitched crying sound. The male may respond by approaching and quivering his own wings. The two mates may touch bills, as if the male were passing food to her. Sometimes he actually does provide her with a tidbit. Then the female crouches down, the male steps up on her back, and the mating is complete.

After mating, the female lays an egg a day until the clutch is complete, usually six eggs. The female does all of the incubating. While she incubates, she needs to eat frequently and gets her food in a variety of ways. Often the male brings her food. He approaches the nest and perches nearby, singing a soft version of the feebee song. The female flies to him and begs, giving a wing quiver and a high-pitched cry. The male feeds her and she returns to the nest. If the male doesn't come soon enough, the female may leave the nest and call to the male to feed her, giving the soft feebee song herself. If he still doesn't come, she will leave the nest briefly and forage for herself. The incubation period is short in chickadees, only about twelve days.

The nesting period is an extension of the incubation period, with subtle differences. The male continues to approach the nest with food, singing his soft song, and the female will fly to him and solicit. But now she solicits for her young, rather than for herself. She wing-quivers, and he flies to the nest and feeds the babies. As the nestlings grow larger she broods them less and begins herself to carry food to the nest. By the end of the nesting period the two parents are sharing the feeding responsibilities about equally. Curiously, the male continues to sing his soft song whenever he approaches the nest. The female always approaches quietly.

At or around sixteen days the young birds leave their nest. For a few weeks they follow the parents closely, demanding and wing-quivering for food. After this fledgling period, the parents no longer feed the young or tolerate them in the territory but drive them off into the no-man's-land between territories. In late summer you can occasionally see the young birds trying to defend little territories of their own. They behave for all the world like children playing at adult roles. They sing inaccurate versions of the feebee song and skirmish over the boundaries of their little temporary territories.

In late summer the chickadees pass through a period of transition, when the adults lose and replace their feathers. During this time the birds are quiet and there is little social activity. Gradually, however, as autumn comes on, the birds begin to form their winter flocks again and defend their winter territories. Neighbors who were bitter enemies only a few weeks before, now begin to travel together from food source to food source, and to defend these food sources against other groups. It is time once again for the gardener to begin filling his feeder.

It has been several minutes now that I have been sitting with my arm out the window, my hand in the glove. Now, suddenly, a chickadee flutters to a nearby twig, pauses, and then flies swiftly to perch on the thumb of the glove. He grabs a seed from the palm of the glove and is gone, his wings whirring like a tiny electric fan. As soon as he leaves, a second bird comes, only to be scared off — before he can grab a seed — by a third bird perching beside him. As the third chickadee is taking his seed, a fourth appears and perches on the window ledge about a foot from the glove.When the third chickadee leaves, the fourth hops into the palm of the glove. This bird is not shy at all but begins to pack his mouth with sunflower seeds — something I have never seen a chickadee do before. Three, four, five — I wouldn't have thought a chickadee's mouth could hold so many seeds. As he shifts in the palm of the glove, I can feel his feet scratching on the leather of the glove, but he is so tiny I can barely feel his weight. I lean forward to study him through the glass of the window until my face is a few inches from his. He lifts his head from his greedy foraging and studies my face boldly. His black eye glistens like a bead in the fuzz of his black cap. He grabs one more seed and flutters off.

My arm is getting cold, my shoulder is stiff, and the room is chilly from having the window open. It is time to see if my experiment has worked. I slip my hand, glove and all, back into the room, remove the glove, put a handful of sunflower seed in the palm of my bare hand,

and put my hand out the window, resting it exactly where the glove had been a moment before. I don't have to wait long. There is a whir of wings and a chickadee is perched on the end of my index finger. I am surprised at how dry and hard, how scaly his tiny feet feel as they wrap my finger in a tight grip. The chickadee seems likewise startled by the new situation. Is it the new shape of the "glove" that alarms him, or does my warm mammalian skin feel strange to him under his toes? He looks up at me quizzically. Then he leans way back on his perch as if to better survey the whole hand. Finally, he grabs a seed and is gone.

At forty-five years of age, I have hand-fed my first chickadee.

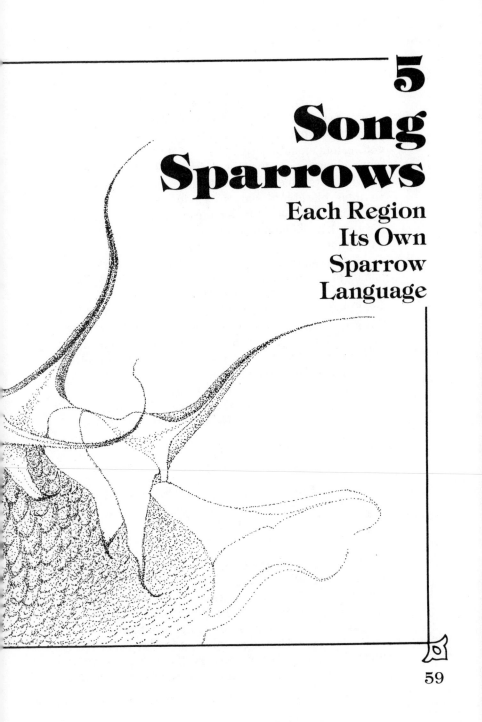

5
Song Sparrows

Each Region
Its Own
Sparrow
Language

It is late February and I am out in the garden searching for a sign of spring. Not the first sign of spring, mind you. We have already had several: the afternoons have been getting longer since early December; the days have been getting longer since the twenty-first of December; we heard the first chickadee songs back in January; and the starlings, blackbirds, and crows reappeared last week. But today I am looking for a more emphatic sign of spring, the sort that will beguile me into thinking that the gardening season is only a few short weeks away.

I stoop and rummage in the rubble of a flower bed, hoping to turn up the tip of a crocus or a snowdrop. There! Is that something green pushing through the brown leaves and litter? No. False hope. My gloved fingers turn up a tiny green plastic tractor, no doubt brought here years ago by some young farmer to help me with the weeding and tilling of the flower bed. Lost, forgotten, buried, it is now heaved to the surface by the frost to fool me into thinking that my early-spring bulbs are starting to come up.

I put the little trophy in my pocket—for what future use I cannot say—and stand looking wistfully out over the brown lawn. And then I hear:

> "Da-da-da
>
> DUH!"

The tune is faint and tangled amid the whinings and peepings of a nearby flock of starlings. Did I really hear it?

> "Da-da-da
>
> DUH!"

There it is again. It's the song I call "Beethoven's Fifth." The bird sings three staccato notes and then a lower, heavier note before his song disintegrates into a tuneless twitter that I cannot follow. The song sounds like the first four notes of Beethoven's Fifth Symphony. Many a musically inclined houseguest has complained about "Beethoven's Fifth" over the years. "I just wish the bird would go on a few bars," a musician friend complained to

me as he helped me weed carrots one late spring morning.
"It's like listening to a student practice the same phrase
over and over again."

But whatever my sophisticated musical friends may
have to say about this song, I am overjoyed to hear it now.
It's the first song sparrow song that I have heard this
season. The song sparrow who sings it owns my garden.
He harvests caterpillars from my cabbage, and sings from
the platform of my raspberry trellis. He is an old friend
and an emphatic harbinger of spring. So far as I am
concerned, he can practice those same four notes of music
as often as he likes.

If your garden is almost anywhere in North America,
chances are it, too, is owned by a song sparrow. If you
don't have a song sparrow in your garden, you have only
yourself to blame. You keep your garden too tidy. The
solution is simple. Just let the place go to seed a bit. You
know those forgotten corners of your yard—too small to
use, too remote to keep up—that tend to get taken over by
chokecherry and goldenrod? Well, that's the sort of
landscape that a song sparrow loves best. If you need an
excuse not to clear up a corner of your yard, just tell
yourself, or your family, or your neighbor, or your city
friends who come to visit that this patch of ground is your
special song sparrow preserve and that you keep it just
like that to encourage the song sparrows. But I don't think
you'll need to do anything special to attract song sparrows.
It's a rare gardener indeed who tends his yard so
fastidiously that a song sparrow can't find a little bushy bit
somewhere in which to hide his nest.

Even if a song sparrow already owns your garden,
you may not recognize your garden's proprietor. Of all the
commonest garden birds, the song sparrow is the most
difficult to recognize. The best time to learn to recognize
song sparrows by sight is not in the summer when they
are nesting and singing, but in the winter when they will
come readily to bird feeders. Look for a smallish brown

61

bird that is streaky all over. It should be a bit bigger than a chickadee or a titmouse or a junco, but a bit smaller than a female red-winged blackbird. The brown should be a dull brown, not a reddish brown. Once you have a streaky brown bird in sight, look closely at its chest. The streaks should cover the entire chest area and should gather together in a spot right at the center of the chest. Look carefully, because song sparrows are not the only brown birds that come to feeders. You will probably see other dull brown birds with a spot in the middle of their chests and still others with streaky chests. But the song sparrow is the only dull brown bird with *both* a streaky chest *and* a spot in the middle of it. Only if your small, streaky brown bird has both of these traits can you be sure that it is a song sparrow.

Fortunately, once you have learned to recognize one adult song sparrow you will always be able to recognize others. Fall, winter, spring, and summer, male or female, all adult sparrows have the same feather pattern. Only the young in the first year differ in not having so streaky a chest and in not having a central spot in the middle of it.

It is more difficult to recognize a song sparrow by its song than by its plumage, because each bird may have as many as two dozen different songs. These are not slight variations on a common theme but are completely different themes. Fortunately, among the songs that each bird sings is usually a group of songs that are helpful in recognizing the bird as a song sparrow. These songs always start with three to six emphasized and tuneful notes that invariably suggest some familiar tune or other. For instance, in a bushy tangle down the road from my house is a song sparrow who sometimes sings:

di
"Da-da   da datwiddle."

After about three weeks of listening to that tune I finally

identified it as "My Country, 'Tis of Thee." (Really, the sparrow sings "thee-ee," but we can't expect the bird to know our patriotic songs exactly.) Down by the river there are two birds, one of which sings "La Cucaracha:"

"da-da-da-DAH da"

and another which sings "Toreador:"

di

"DAH   da-da da."

So, if you find yourself listening to a bird who begins his song with a few bars from some familiar tune, but who stubbornly refuses to finish it, that bird is probably a song sparrow.

The way to learn to recognize song sparrows by their songs is to practice on a bird you know for sure is a song sparrow. Take a lawn chair down to the end of your garden and sit yourself down comfortably with a pair of binoculars, a glass of iced tea, and perhaps a bottle of bug repellent in case the mosquitoes find you. Be patient and don't fidget too much, and pretty soon your song sparrow should be along. He'll alight on the top of a nearby bush, the tip of a bean pole, or the roof peak of a shed, puff up his chest, and begin to sing. Look in the middle of that puffed-up chest for the stripes converging in a spot. Once you're sure he's a song sparrow, keep track of him as he goes about his business. When he's in a mood to sing, he will be easy to keep track of. He will fly from perch to perch, often changing the tune he is singing just about the time he changes his perch. From each perch he'll give you several renditions of one of his songs before flying on to another perch and giving several renditions of another song. He'll keep it up until eventually he runs through his whole repertoire of songs. It's almost as if he's trying to teach you his repertoire.

Despite the wide variety of tunes, as you listen you will begin to get a feel for what is the common theme in all song sparrow songs. I wish I could simply tell you what that theme is instead of making you find it out for yourself, but although I can usually recognize song sparrow song in the field without any difficulty, I can't say *how* I do it. The song has some distinctive feature, something about the quality of the notes, something about the rhythm, something about the manner in which the song is divided into different sorts of notes. What it is, I just can't say. But I can say that if you are willing to let your song sparrow teach you, before very long you will be able to recognize the song sparrow songs in your part of the country, just as well as I can recognize those in mine.

The relationship between the song sparrow's song and his society is among the most interesting in the bird world. It's one of those natural phenomena that becomes more and more puzzling and intriguing the more you know about it.

When we humans think about animals, we tend to assign to them ways of thinking that we glean from our dealings with our fellow human beings. In other words, we anthropomorphize the animal. It's only natural to do so. In fact, it's probably a good thing, since we wouldn't be quite so interested in animals if we didn't think that what they did had something to do with what we ourselves do. But while anthropomorphism helps to interest us in animals, it can also lead to misinterpretation of their behavior, in the same way that assuming other *people* do things for the same reasons we do can lead to misinterpretations. Some scientists say that we should never anthropomorphize when we think about animals, but I think that's throwing out the baby with the bath water. I think it's best to take a middle course, to let ourselves anthropomorphize, but to be constantly wary of error and to carefully compare our interpretations with what the animal is doing to see if our anthropomorphisms are accurate.

Take for example the idea of "territory" to describe relations among neighboring song sparrows. Whenever anyone uses the term *territory* concerning animals, I find I always apply to it my stereotype of a California suburban subdivision. I see in my mind geometric plots laid out in a monotonous plan, each plot defended by its owner against each other plot-holder. I see the various plot-holders as having no relationship to one another except the aggressive defense of their boundaries. I think of their songs as a proclamation of rights, as if California subdivision homeowners were to step to their hedges at dawn each morning and shout, "I AM MALCOLM T. HOUSEHOLDER OF 220803 BELLA TERRAZZIO LANE, NOVA MUNDIA, CALIFORNIA 94706. I HAVE A TWENTY-YEAR MORTGAGE, A WIFE, TWO BEAUTIFUL CHILDREN, A POOL, AND TWO CARS—AND I'LL FIGHT TO THE DEATH ANY MAN WHO TRIES TO TAKE ANY OF IT AWAY FROM ME!"

Leaving aside the question of whether this caricature is fair to Californians, we should agree that it isn't fair to song sparrows. "Neighborhood" rather than "subdivision" is a much better way to describe how song sparrows in adjacent territories behave toward one another. The fact is that even though neighboring male song sparrows dispute with one another over boundaries and mates, they also share things and have common interests. The song sparrows of a given neighborhood share, for instance, a distaste for birds of prey, and will gather to scold if such a bird threatens one of their territories. The birds of a neighborhood may share family ties, too. The song sparrow in your garden doubtless has a few close relatives living nearby in the neighborhood—a son or daughter of a previous year, a brother or sister, a father still maintaining a territory in the area, or perhaps a grandchild prospecting among the territories of the neighborhood for a space in which to set himself up and begin to sing. In a song sparrow neighborhood, neighbors may even share space. They may give ground more gracefully or at least defend space less tenaciously against familiar neighbors than

65

against strangers who wander in from the outside and attempt to claim a territory.

But the most spectacular example of sharing among the birds of a song sparrow neighborhood is the sharing of bits and pieces of song. Your song sparrow will have about a dozen songs, each of which is unique to him in detail. But the elements of those songs, the pieces of which they are made, will be widely shared among the other song sparrows of the neighborhood. Certainly that is true in my song sparrow neighborhood. The song element I call Beethoven's Fifth, which is sung by the bird in my garden, is also sung by many other birds on the farm. There's a bird down by the river who sings it, and another in the north pasture. Each sings the theme in his own way and with a different ending, but the basic pattern of the first four notes is definitely the same. Similarly, "My Country, 'Tis of Thee," "La Cucaracha," and "Toreador" can each be heard at more than one place in the neighborhood.

When you think about the singing of song sparrows in this way, it becomes more like a community sing-along or a "hootenanny" than a bunch of bad neighbors shouting at each other over their fences. As each bird flies from perch to perch, he may address to his nearest neighbor a song similar to the song that neighbor has been singing. What follows is like a game of "Name That Tune." The lead bird tries out new tunes and his neighbor follows with the tune in his repertoire that is most similar. As soon as the second bird picks up this tune, the lead bird changes to another, as if to say, "O.K., you got that one, but how about *this* one!?" Scientists don't know for sure if song sparrows hold hootenannies, but it certainly sounds like it when I'm listening to the song sparrows singing on my farm.

How the members of a neighborhood of song sparrows come by all their songs, nobody knows for sure. Young birds, even before they are able to fly, are capable

of learning something about the songs in their neighborhood. The birds seem to pick up their songs during the
first fall and first spring of their lives by improvising and
by listening to neighbors' songs. You can sometimes hear
them "practicing." Their song is indistinct and ill-formed
at first, like the babbling of babies. But in time it develops
into adult song, and by the time a bird's first brood is born
he will have learned or improvised all the songs he will
ever sing in his life. Many of the bits and pieces of his
song will be those borrowed from his neighbors and
modified to suit his own taste.

Why do the song sparrows invest so much effort in
learning songs? Scientists more or less agree that nature
strives to be economical. They also agree—more or
less—that birds' songs are designed to convey three types
of information: the species identity of the singer (so that
males may be warned that there is a potential competitor
in the neighborhood and females may be advised that
there is a potential mate), his personal identity (so that
females may know that they are listening to their mate
and territorial neighbors may know that they are listening
to a familiar competitor), and finally, his eagerness to mate
or to defend his territory (so that potential rivals and
potential mates may compare the singer's motivations to
their own). All this is successfully communicated by song
sparrow song. Once you have some experience with song
sparrows, you will be able to identify a singer as a song
sparrow, a particular song sparrow, and a song sparrow in
a particular mood. If you can do it, presumably other song
sparrows can, too. Clearly the song sparrow's song does
its job.

But compared to the songs of some other birds, the
song sparrow's song appears to do its job rather badly.
The song sparrow has a very close cousin with habits
that are similar in many respects. If you have spent time in
the north woods of Canada or perhaps along the crest of

67

the Appalachian Mountains, you will know this bird well. He is called the white-throated sparrow, and his song consists of several unmistakable, clear-toned whistles whose cadence mimics the cadence of the spoken phrase "Old Sam Peabody, Peabody, Peabody." The "Old Sam" part consists of long clear tones, and the "Peabodies" of triplets of little short tones. The point is that every white-throated song sparrow sings this song and *only* this song. Each bird sings a slightly different variant of it, the differences between variants being in the exact pitches of the tones in the "Old Sam" part of the song. From occasion to occasion an individual bird will vary his performance, but only in the number of "Peabodies" he sings; the more Peabodies, the more eager is the singer to defend his territory.

By comparison with the song sparrow, the song of the white-throated sparrow seems a marvel of natural efficiency. With a few clear tones the bird is able to convey all that a bird needs to say about himself: his membership in a particular species, his individual identity, and his readiness to defend his territory. Given the efficiency of the white-throated sparrow's song, it is curious that the song sparrow goes to such elaborate lengths to convey the same information. More curious still is the fact that the song sparrow's song is so inefficient as a means of communication. While it takes only a few songs from a white-throated sparrow for the message to get through, it takes several song sparrow songs to convey the same information, unless the hearer is very familiar with the song sparrow songs of a particular neighborhood. So why does a song sparrow go to such elaborate ends to do badly what a white-throated sparrow does more effectively and with less effort?

Whenever I am casting around in my mind for an anthropomorphism to help me with this puzzle, I keep coming back to the hootenanny. A hootenanny is a gathering of musicians for the purpose of performing and trading folk songs. The idea of a hootenanny is for each musician to try to come up with more obscure songs or obscure versions of songs than anybody else in the room. The reward for "winning" is that you get to teach your song to the other musicians in the room, who gather round to hear the words of the song and crane their necks to see the fingering of the chords.

Now if you asked me how come the members of a hootenanny know so many songs, the answer would be obvious. Since the object of the competition is to know more songs than anybody else, each time the musicians get together, more songs are sung. It works like this: Let's say that at the first "hoot" most of the singers know three songs but one singer knows four. The singer who knows four will teach his unique song to the other participants in the hoot so that the next time they meet, everybody will know at least four songs. Between meetings of the hoot, somebody in the group will learn or make up a new song or two and that person will teach those songs to the other musicians at the next hoot. In this way, the competition of the hoot leads the repertoires of the singers to get bigger and bigger until they strain the limits of the memories of the singers.

Now I'm not suggesting that the "community sing" of song sparrows is exactly like a hootenanny. There are some obvious differences. For one thing, song sparrows learn songs only when they are young. Furthermore, an individual song sparrow doesn't sing against all singers at once, but usually against one neighbor at a time as they meet across territorial boundaries. But what I am suggesting is that a system of competition in which the winner is the individual who sings just one more song eventually leads to everybody's knowing a great many songs, and that a song sparrow neighborhood may engender such a competition. If this is true, then we don't

69

have to explain why song sparrows sing a dozen songs. We have only to explain why it is that a song sparrow would want to sing one more song than his neighbor. Once we know the answer to that question, the rules of the hoot will take care of the rest.

Unfortunately, we don't know the answer to that question. If, by watching the song sparrows in your garden, you can figure out what advantage comes to the singer of more songs, then you will have learned something that scientists have only guessed at up till now.

In my own garden the Beethoven's Fifth song has been sung for as long as I have lived at the farm—almost twelve years. I like to think that my garden has been owned all that time by a single Methuselah of a song sparrow and his wife, raising brood after brood, year after year. Or at least I like to think that I have been listening to generations of offspring of the original singer of Beethoven's Fifth who greeted me when I first came to the farm twelve years ago. But when I am sensible, I have to recognize that it is more likely that the Beethoven's Fifth singer is a different bird each year, not directly related to the bird who sang that same theme from that same bush the summer before.

The sad fact is that a song sparrow's life is a tough and chancy one. Of all the song sparrows who breed in my neighborhood in a particular year, only about half can be expected to survive to the following breeding season. Of those, only half will return to the same territory. Thus, the chances that any particular song sparrow has presided over my garden for more than a few of those twelve years are very small. And even if the same male returned, the chances that he mated with the same female are negligible. It is rare for song sparrow mates to find each other again a second season.

The chances are even more remote that any of the adult offspring of my original breeding pair ever came back to my garden. True, that first pair might have had a great many descendants. Once a pair begins to breed in April, they can reel off three or four broods of about four offspring in a single summer. Some pairs will survive to breed another year—usually with a different mate. All together, two song sparrows can expect to produce about twenty eggs during their lifetime. If all of those eggs of my original pair had hatched and the fledglings had been as fortunate as their parents and all their offspring had hatched and so forth until now, then my original pair of song sparrows would have had millions of direct descendants by now—surely enough to assure me of at least one for my garden.

But young song sparrows lead such a perilous life that I would be lucky if any of those descendants ever returned to breed in my garden. Only about half the eggs ever produce young that fledge; the rest are destroyed by other birds, mammals, and gardeners who are overzealous about clearing up the brushy corners of their yards. Of those young sparrows that do make it out of the nest, only two—on the average—ever survive to breed. Because of the same perils, these two birds can be expected to have but two offspring over their lifetime. Thus, despite the enormous reproductive potential of song sparrows, they barely manage to replace themselves. Furthermore, if there are lineal descendants of my original birds in the neighborhood, I can't count on them to be on their ancestors' territory. Song sparrow offspring will often return to the general area from which they were fledged, but they rarely return to the same territory.

In short, I'm lucky if I have a distant relative of my original Beethoven's Fifth bird in my garden, far less the same bird or a direct descendant.

My tenacious belief that it is the same song sparrow singing in my garden each year is the result of a misleading anthropomorphism. We human beings are a very special sort of animal. Our lives are long. We care for, protect, and attend to each individual child. We expect to survive year after year and we expect our children to live and grow up and bear us grandchildren. More often than not our expectations are fulfilled. Tenuous as human life sometimes seems to be, it is steel riveted in granite compared with the life of a song sparrow.

I can hear the Beethoven's Fifth theme clearly now. It appears to be coming from the northwest corner of my garden, from the top of a shriveled sunflower stalk that I left standing for the blue jays last fall.

"Da-da-da
DUH."

The sound transforms me. Only a moment ago I was a weary, middle-aged man standing in the middle of a disreputable lawn with a silly plastic tractor in my pocket. Now I am an organic gardener. My mind darts around the yard, looking for things to be done. I can drive the corner post of the garden and measure it out. I can get the tiller out and change its oil. I can call my neighbor and arrange to have the manure spread. There is no time to be lost. In a few short weeks it will be time to plant the peas and the spinach. Why did I wait so long to order the seeds? If I do it today, perhaps I can still get the preseason discount.

As I start back toward the house a curious thing happens. With its odd, fluttering, bounding flight, the song sparrow flies from the sunflower head directly toward me. It is almost as if he has seen me and is coming to greet me. At the last moment he veers aside and perches at the tip of a nearby peach tree. He puffs up his chest, showing clearly his brown streaks and spot.

He sings:

di
"Da da   da datwiddle."

It's the "My Country, 'Tis of Thee" theme. It is hard to describe the pleasure I feel at being greeted by this little fellow. I want to return the greeting to the bird in some way, to shake his hand, to throw my arms about him, to say "How was your winter, old fellow? Where did you go? What did you see? Do you remember all the things that happened last summer? Do you remember when the tiller bent your nest bush and we had to prop it upright? Are you glad to be back?"

But I have to remember that even though it sings the same songs, it's probably not the same bird. Possibly a neighbor from last year, prospecting my garden to see if he wants to take it over this year. Possibly a distant relative. Possibly even a complete stranger, a first-year bird from another neighborhood. Last year's bird has probably died or relocated. Among song sparrows—as among most birds—the lives of individuals are evanescent and inconsequential. Only the music is eternal.

6
Robins
Tuneful
Aggression

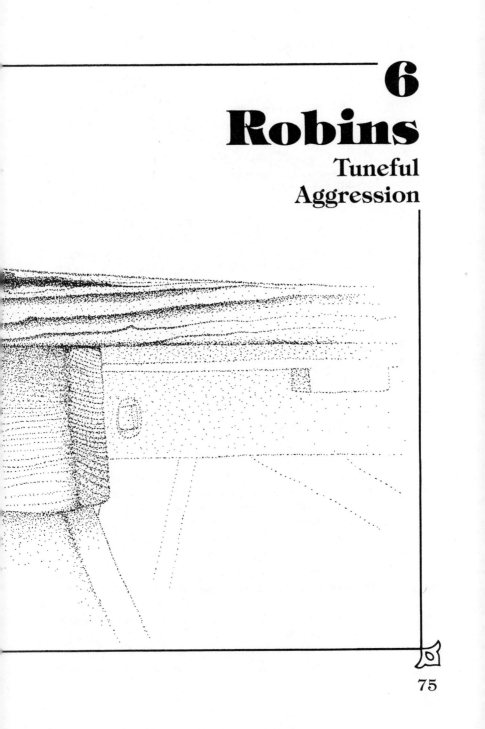

It is the Sunday following the change to Daylight Saving Time, and I am out taking an after-dinner stroll with my robins. Ah, Daylight Saving Time, that seasonal celebration of the capacity of the human species to delude itself! We wish to arise early and have the benefit of the morning sun, to be up and get the early worm. We know, in an individualistic society like ours, that we could never legislate such virtue. But it's no fun being virtuous alone.

So what do we do? We change time itself. At 2 A.M. on Saturday night, we send rockets with giant pincers to grasp the globe and wrench it back one twenty-fourth of its rotation. During the night, as we sleep, the oceans slosh violently back and forth in their basins, and gales swoosh around the world as the atmosphere is thrown forward by its momentum. Mountains quake and the stars halt their progression. For a moment, it is as if the universe will fly apart. But we never see these grand events. Before we wake, the atmosphere and the oceans calm themselves, the mountain ranges settle their ruffled feathers, and the sun miraculously rises—exactly an hour later. For another summer, the forces of nature have bowed to mankind's wish to see a bit more of the sun.

If the robins could know of our self-delusion, of our manipulativeness and credulity, they would think us wonderfully absurd. As it is, they are merely puzzled to find me outside at an hour when they expect to have the garden to themselves. They fly up from the lawn, protesting. Their "perp-perp" calls rise in speed, loudness, and harshness as I approach, "perp . . . . . . perp . . . . perp . . . perp . . perp pink pink PINK!" I confess that I am also a bit puzzled to find myself out in the garden. Now that we are on the new time, the slant rays of the sun streaming in from the northwest, the columns of shadow laid across the lawn by the trunks of the oak and cherry tree to the side of the garden look to me like an *August* scene. This kind of light at this time of day reminds me of warm late-summer evenings when I have dozens of gardening chores to perform. But the bare trees, the empty garden, and the shabby lawn all suggest a late-fall or early-winter landscape. Dirty rags of snow litter the ground on the shaded north side of the barn. An icewater wind blows down the valley. The evening chatter of the frogs has slowed to an occasional lonesome peep. Only the garden rows tilled for the peas and spinach give any hint of the season. I long to fetch my hoe and seeds and plant something more, but I know I must be patient. Nothing else will grow in a soil so cold. Next week I'll try the beets and the chard, but tonight there's nothing to do but wait.

These melancholy thoughts have brought me to a standstill. I zip up my jacket and shiver. The robins have stopped their perping and returned to the ground. In their foraging, each pursues a pattern of dignified caution: hop-hop-hop, pause, stand upright, peck, peck, swallow, pause, stand upright, hop-hop-hop. Mostly the birds hop straight ahead, but sometimes when an individual finds a particularly luscious worm or grub, his hopping pattern changes. He begins to crisscross the same bit of ground, as if hoping to turn up the brothers and sisters of the worm he has just found. He catches a few more and resumes his straight-line hopping across the lawn. If two robins' straight paths intersect, they veer off from one another. To show one's red breast to another robin is to invite a squabble, and few robins have time for a squabble on such a cold spring evening. Now one of the robins flies up to the top of the cherry tree and begins to sing "cheerily-cheerup ..... cheerily ..... cheerily ..... cheerup." The pace is very languid, the silences long. It is a cold sound, which seems to echo off the hard surfaces of the buildings and the boughs of the leafless trees. August sunlight or no, winter still grips this land.

Back inside the warm house, I find the robins are still on my mind. The male robin is the *Bürgermeister* of the

77

bird world. Dignified in his bearing, respectable in his family habits, obsessively concerned with the security of his lands and his family, everything about the robin suggests gentry. Even his dress—sober grey long coat revealing a plush orange shirt in front—suggests a man who wants simultaneously to assert his respectability and his awareness of style. The American robin is much more properly our national bird than is the bald eagle. The bald eagle is representative of America's predatory and scavaging frontier past. The robin represents our conservative, contemporary present. He's the bird of Main Street—neither the struggling downtown part of Main Street nor the part on the outskirts of town where it threads its way past gas stations and restaurants and passes under the interstate. The robins' world is the part of Main Street that passes through comfortable neighborhoods where quiet lawns stretch out under the shade of oaks and maples and perhaps even the delicate fronds of an elm. Here the robins strut on the lawns and protest indignantly at any disturbance to their domain.

The fortunes of the robin have been intimately tied to how Americans live. Before the settlers came from Europe, it's hard to imagine how the robins got on. Robins are thrushes, a family of birds that makes its living mostly in forests. The hermit thrush, the wood thrush, the veery, the grey-cheeked thrush—their names bring to mind haunting tunes echoing around the trunks of tall trees in the mosquito-ridden depths of dank forests. In precolonial America the robin must have been a specialist adapted to exploit the clearings of these forests, perhaps the meadows along the banks of rivers where winter flooding and summer grazing kept the trees at bay and mud for nests was plentiful. Such clearings must have been few and far between in precolonial America, and the robin must have been among the rarest of birds. But as soon as the colonists began to cut the forests and introduce sheep, horses, and cattle, then the robins must have come into their own. And as the settlers spread west, acre by acre, the robin's domain replaced that of his deep-woods cousins until nowadays he is the best-known of American birds and the only thrush that most people are familiar with.

The first part of the twentieth century saw a bit of a dip in the fortunes of robins, at least in the East. All up and down the Eastern seaboard, tractors replaced draft animals, dairy farms were consolidated, and pasturage decreased. Fewer and fewer became the well-grazed, well-manured pastures with watering springs or troughs that robins so favor. More and more common became the forests of white pine and scrub pine hardwood saplings where a robin was hard-pressed to find a living.

But since the Second World War, the future of the robin has been assured by the coming of the power mower and the lawn sprinkler. If a convention of the robin species had commissioned humanity to provide for them, the outcome could not have been more to the liking of robins. The well-watered ground, the frequent mowing, the short, lush grass that typify new American suburbs are exactly what a robin needs to live well. Modern life hasn't hurt the robin a bit; in fact, the winter range of the robin seems to be spreading north and west from the Eastern coastline.

We should be grateful for the resilience of our robins, because modern life has not been so kind to the robin's beautiful cousin, the bluebird. Once almost as abundant as the robin, this gentle, soft-spoken little bird is now rare. The birds are so similar in their habits that it's hard to see why civilization should have been so hard on one and so easy on the other. Both are monogamous, territorial songbirds, who migrate from the southern United States to the North each year. Both are highly dependent on berries and other wild fruit as survival food in the winter and suffer terribly if large-scale southern ice storms seal up their food supply. Both like open country better than the woodland habitats favored by their thrush cousins. In fact, the bluebird seems a little less fussy than the robin in his choice of habitat. The bluebird is a sort of an insect hawk, who sits on perches and pounces on insects in the grass. For his way of life he doesn't need the flat-grazed pastures or well-manicured lawns; he'll take a scrubby orchard or overgrown pasture. He'll sit on the trailing tips of one of the apple tree limbs, watching the grass for signs of movement, and displaying his wonderful blue feathers against the pink and white of the apple blossoms. It's a breathtaking sight, but one I have not seen since my childhood.

Similar as the two birds are, there is one disastrous difference between them. The bluebird is a hole nester. To be a hole nester is to compete with other birds for a scarce resource for one's nest site. Suitable nesting cavities are in short supply. Unless you are a woodpecker, you have to wait until a woodpecker abandons a hole or until a knot in a tree rots and forms a cavity in the tree. The competition is ferocious and the competitors include some of the most ruthless thugs of the bird world. For example, house wrens are not only ferociously tenacious in securing a nesting hole for their own young, they are spiteful as well. They patrol all the potential nesting holes within their territory and try to break the eggs of any hole nester that uses a hole they themselves aren't using. Worse still are the starlings and English sparrows. The persistence of these cavity nesters is legendary, and unless the cavity's dimension is precisely suited to the needs of the bluebird, it will be the starling or the English sparrow that will get the hole. Civilization did the bluebird a great injustice when it unleashed small populations of these European birds on the eastern United States. But fortunately for robin watchers, the invasion of America by English sparrows has had relatively little effect on the populations of robins.

If you have a large, well-kept lawn and you don't have one or more pairs of robins nesting within a few feet of your house, I'd be surprised. Robins come by the dozen to inspect such a robin paradise and to dispute who is to occupy it. So attached are the birds to humans that they sometimes give up tree nesting altogether in favor of nesting in parts of your house: atop a sheltered decorative pillar, inside an open porch, anyplace that is sheltered and safe from predators.

Given how closely robins live among us, it's amazing that we know as little about them as we do. This ignorance of the wild creatures that share our yards and lawns with us seems almost like a form of politeness. Where I live, when one neighbor wants to praise another he often says, "He's a good neighbor; he minds his own business." If you live in the country, you know that your life is laid bare for all who would drive slowly by your door to see. To an experienced rural resident, a glance at your yard tells volumes — the clothes on the line, the cars in the dooryard, the number of rooms lighted, the height of the grass, the number of heifers in the pasture, the comings and goings of the milk truck — each detail reveals an intimacy: the ebbing and flowing of financial fortunes, the coming and goings of guests and family members, sickness, health, good fortune and bad. It is the genius of country neighbors that they don't take the opportunities offered to figure out what's going on next door; or if they do, they keep their inferences to themselves.

The nice thing about our animal neighbors is that we can be as nosy as we like and it doesn't hurt anybody. The nice thing about robins is that you can be nosy without even leaving your front veranda. Sitting on the porch swing with your feet up on the rail and a glass of lemonade at your side, you can learn all the secrets of robin life. If you have a little patience and persistence, patterns will gradually begin to emerge.

Unless your porch swing is in a particularly well-sheltered and sunny location, the first stage in the robin's breeding cycle is likely to pass you by. Sometime in late April or early May the male robins begin to get serious about territory. Up until then their song is sporadic and the birds still feed in loose flocks, but as the weather warms, individuals begin to claim territories of an acre or so and try to exclude flocks and neighbors from their domain. A territory claimant sings loudly and continuously. He may fly at a trespasser if one forages on his lawn. The two birds may actually scuffle, leaping into the air chest to chest and battering at each other with wings, claws, and beaks. Soon you will notice that instead of groups of robins on your lawn, you are seeing only one or two at a time. And unless these are a mated pair of birds, you can bet that any two robins you will see on your lawn will be feeding on opposite ends of it.

Pair formation and mating are easy to miss. The key to the relationship between a male and a female robin is territory. Mostly the male defends it and the female raises young on it. The male advertises for a mate by singing. One moment you will notice that your male robin is singing a great deal; the next moment, there is a female sitting beside him on the branch. Mating is equally perfunctory. You will notice the male attending the female, perhaps even pestering her, as she goes about the territory feeding. She may become irritable and may even charge him, her head down, her beak open. But eventually she becomes receptive, and when she does, mating occurs so quickly you will have to be alert to see it. He approaches. She crouches. He mounts, fluttering and fanning his tail, and the deed is done. Sometimes mating is more amicable. One mating described to me proceeded as follows: The male flew to the short grass of a well-grazed bit of pasture and began to sing. The female joined him there and the two pecked for a few moments gently at each other's bills. The male mounted, they mated, and then the two flew up to the tree where the nest was to be built. That was it! That was courtship in the robin.

If you missed territory selection, pair formation, and mating, don't worry. You won't miss nest building. The first thing you will probably notice is that the robins begin to take an inordinate interest in mud puddles. The female — she's slightly paler and less showy in her plumage than her mate — will make repeated trips from the mud puddle to a particular bush or cornice on your house where a rough platform of sticks and stems has already been built. Each load of mud she brings she presses into the platform and molds into a cup shape with vigorous movements of her body and feet. When the cup is built, she lines it with some soft material, often fine grasses, to protect the eggs and also to insulate them. My robins used to favor the tufts of horse fur that littered the pasture from the late-winter shedding of the pony's coat. Since we sold the pony, the robins have had to settle for dog fur or even for the products of a family haircutting session, held on the lawn on a warm spring day.

What your male robin will do while your female is building her nest seems to vary from individual to individual, or from place to place. Different naturalists have observed different behaviors. Some say that the male helps the female construct the nest. They agree that he is not as efficient at building as the female and that mostly he brings the materials and drops them carelessly on the nest for the female to work in. But other observers have seen different and more puzzling behavior on the part of the male. As the female goes back and forth from the nest site to the place where mud or grass or stems are being foraged, the male alternates two behaviors. On one trip he will accompany her to the pasture and shepherd her as she goes about selecting bits of material. He never picks up any materials himself; he just seems to watch

83

over her. During her next trip, however, he remains in the nest tree and sings. The alternation is strange because you would think that if the female is at risk when she is in the pasture he would accompany her on each trip. Or if his territory is in danger of being lost, he should stay and guard it. Why these male robins so rigidly alternate between singing and guarding is a puzzle. It's as if they share their time between two terribly important tasks, each of which they dare not neglect for too long or too often: the protection of their mates and the defense of their territories.

Nest building takes but a few days, and only a few days after the nest is complete the eggs are laid and incubation begins. Now the robin's life settles down into an unmistakable routine. For most of the time the female sits on the eggs. She sits very still and doesn't move unless a predator or some other source of disturbance comes very close. Every so often she will get up, stand at the edge of the nest, and rotate the eggs.

But if she is to make heat for the eggs, she must feed herself, so once or twice an hour she flies down to the grass to hunt for food. The male, who may have been foraging or singing at some distant part of the territory, now returns to the nest tree to sit within sight of the nest and sing his song. During the male's nest-guarding song, he is very aggressive. If any bird comes near the nest, it is likely to be chased vigorously, and if caught is pecked and battered with blows from the robin's wings. These male bouts of song are short, lasting about five minutes or so, and very regular. On cold days, when the female doesn't dare leave the nest, the bouts will be shorter and less frequent. On warm days they will be longer and more frequent. When the female returns from feeding, she goes immediately to the nest and the male returns to his foraging or territorial patrol.

If you are out about in your garden when robins have eggs in the nest, their routine will give this fact away immediately. First the male is on the lawn, strutting and feeding, and then suddenly he is gone. Now you hear his song from near the nest site. Now the female appears, vigorously foraging for worms. The song continues. Then suddenly it stops. You look up from your work. The female is gone. The male has returned to his feeding. This routine will carry on for about two weeks, until the young are hatched.

The hatching is revealed in another dramatic change in the behavior of the parents. Within a few days the female stops her brooding and the male his singing and the two parents devote an enormous amount of time carrying food to the nest. The young birds will grow from creatures as big as the bowl of a teaspoon to full-grown robins in only thirteen days. Over this time period the parents have to bring about a pound of food to the nest for each of the three to four nestlings and carry away a prodigious quantity of fecal matter. All this must be accomplished while guarding the babies against predators and eating enough food to keep themselves in good condition. Between the two parents, they will make upward of thirty trips to the nest a day bearing food, mostly earthworms and insect larvae. On most outward-bound journeys, the parents will carry and dispose of one of the neat white packages of fecal material that the young have conveniently deposited at the edge of the nest.

The young will have pinfeathers in a few days, be fully feathered in a few more, be ready to leave the nest if necessary in ten days, and will be gone in thirteen. All in all, the period of development between hatching and fledging seems to be conducted in a horrendous rush—as if the parents feared for the lives of their nestlings. And in fact, the danger is very real. With all the activity around the nest, it is a dull-witted cat or squirrel that will not begin to notice that there is a nest nearby and begin to plot a raid on it. Until the young robins leave the nest and scatter, the parents run the risk of losing the entire brood to a single accident, whether it be a predator or a bad windstorm or a spring downpour that erodes the nest.

That a nest is a dangerous place for a young robin to stay for too long may explain why the youngsters seem to leave the nest so ill-prepared for independent life. The departure of young robins from the nests near my house always seems to be the occasion for excitement. Inevitably the dogs and the cats get themselves involved. The young robins flutter around, losing altitude on every trip, and blunder and bang into things. The cat races about, trying to grasp them with his outstretched claws. The children chase the cat, reprimanding it loudly. The dog wags his tail and barks. I, the natural historian, stand by and shout instructions. The parent robins "pink-pink" as loudly and shrilly as they can and dive-bomb all the other participants in the game, no matter which side they are on. Cat, dog, children, and natural historian—all are in danger of being pecked.

It is a rare fledging day in which one of the baby robins is not lost. Guerilla warrior that he is, the cat usually gets his way in the end. The parent robins concentrate their efforts on feeding the strong fledglings that are higher in the tree. The children tire of their role as protectors. The dog wanders off to his cool place under the porch. And the cat waits, tail by his side, paws folded under his chest—eyes turned patiently skyward, watching for whatever may befall him.

The next week or so in the lives of the robins is a period of transition. After the perilous first few hours of the fledging period, the responsibilities of caring for the young now fall primarily to the male. You will see him out on the lawn pursued by one or two of the fat, spotted babies, alternately trying to feed for themselves and rushing over to their parent to beg a morsel he may have turned up. Meanwhile, the female feeds herself, recoups her strength, and soon will be found searching the lawns, pastures, and mud puddles for bits of nesting material again. The male, when he is not shepherding young, reasserts his claim over his territory. Once again he engages in long bouts of song. Once again the two parents court and mate, and the cycle begins again. They will repeat it once, perhaps twice more, in the season that still lies ahead.

Your porch swing is an excellent vantage point from which to answer some interesting scientific questions about the robin's life history. Scientists know remarkably little about the robin's natural history, perhaps because scientists behave like nosy and intrusive strangers. They lurk near nests in little tents or they follow the birds around, pointing things at them: first a pair of binoculars, now a telescope, finally — worst of all — a microphone with a long barrel that looks like a shotgun. You may not have all the wonderful equipment the scientist has, but you have one great advantage. You are a good country neighbor. You are busy about your garden, but you rarely focus your attention directly on the bird. Birds are very sensitive when they are the object of human attention. Walk briskly along a path in a city park and the robins will pay you no heed. But pause for a minute to study them, and they will become edgy and even fly off. So it's to your credit with your robins that you are frequently seen, yet mostly preoccupied with your own affairs. Your robins may show things to you that they would not so readily reveal to a scientist. You might, for instance, learn some things about the robin's song that scientists don't know yet, just from sitting on your porch swing.

You might, for instance, use your porch swing as a vantage point from which to ponder the mating habits of robins. As befits a representative of Middle America, the robin is a monogamist. Because monogamy is the norm in American society, we tend to find nothing surprising about the monogamy of robins. But not all birds are monogamists, by any means. In fact, many of the field birds that inhabit our pastures and meadows are polygamists—each male having several mates—as we shall see in the chapter on blackbirds. In fact, there is a theory favored by some scientists that suggests all birds should be polygamous. So you see, the monogamy of robins, suitable as it seems to our Middle American eyes, may require explanation.

The idea that a male robin should have more than one mate arises from noticing a curious asymmetry in the relationship among the sexes in birds. The contribution of males and females to the reproductive process are very different. The female contributes an egg, an object that represents a substantial portion of her body weight; a male contributes only a bit of sperm. As a consequence of this difference in what they contribute to a fertilized egg, the male and female may have slightly different interests in it. Natural selection would not usually reward a female for neglecting her eggs in one nest by attempting to lay eggs in another because so much effort on her part would be required to produce an additional brood of eggs. But it just might reward a male to neglect his female and her eggs in order to assist a second female to begin a second brood on his behalf. It costs him just a moment of time and a few milligrams of sperm. Now if each of these females were able to raise a brood with the diluted assistance of such a bigamous male, then such a male would have twice as many offspring as a monogamous male—a real triumph in biological terms.

So the question is posed: Why don't we have more bigamous robins? One answer is that we may have bigamous robins more often than we think. The solicitous way in which a courting male robin follows his female mate around when he senses she may be ready to mate may be very wise. The fact is that a neighbor male robin, seeing a female next door in a receptive frame of mind and not attended by her male, has been known to swoop in and mate with her. Thus, the babies raised and guarded by the male who owns the territory may not be his babies. To raise another male's offspring is a major calamity in biological terms. Small wonder, therefore, that a male robin should follow so closely his female when he thinks she may be ready to mate.

But why don't male robins neglect their females as soon as the eggs are hatched and put at least some of their time into finding a second mate? If you once watch the raising of a brood of robin babies from eggs to fledglings, my guess is that the answer will be obvious to you. The fact is that both parents must spend every waking minute feeding the nestlings if they are to fledge on time. The male does not seek other females because if he did, the babies in his own first nest would very likely die. While occasionally single parents have been known to rear broods of robins, the chances of succeeding are not good. Raising baby robins is a put-and-take proposition: the more fed, the faster raised. And with each passing day, the searching predators are more likely to locate the nest. This desperate race-against-the-clock aspect of raising baby robins ensures the father's fidelity. Better one brood in a bush than two inside the stomach of a cat.

Another use for your porch swing vantage point is to figure out what the robins' calls and songs signify. Scientists, for instance, have only a vague notion about what a robin's song means. They know that the song consists of at least two kinds of phrases, cheerilys and cheerups. But they don't know the difference in the meaning of a song with lots of cheerilys and a song with lots of cheerups. After half a dozen long sessions on your porch swing, you may be able to answer that question for yourself. Keep track of the cheerilys and cheerups as you also notice what the robin is doing and what's going on around him. If there's room on the porch swing for a notebook and a watch with a sweep second hand, you might want to bring them along and take a few notes. If you marked down separate "minutes" and then noted the number of cheerilys, the number of cheerups, and all the things that the robin did or that happened in that minute, I bet after a few evenings on the swing you would begin to notice some pattern—more cheerilys to cheerups when the mate is near, or more cheerups to cheerilys when another male robin is singing, or some such pattern. Once you have discovered a pattern like this, you would have come a long way toward making up your own personal, unique, scientific, porch swing hypothesis about the meaning of robin song.

You might even solve the mystery of the perp-perp vocalizations. Sometimes the reason for the perps is obvious. The louder, faster, and more strident the perps, the nearer is the cat, the closer to the ground is the fledgling, and the more excited are the parents. The effects of the perp-perp calls are also sometimes evident. A foraging female robin will fly up to the nest when she hears her mate perping. Or a fledgling robin, which a moment before was peeping and fluttering piteously in the grass, will crouch motionless and silent when its parents begin to perp overhead. But sometimes the robins seem to perp and pink for no good reason. Many summer evenings the robin in the lilac bush near my study window perps and pinks all evening until the light has faded from the sky. I look to see if the cat is up to some mischief or if there is an owl about, but all seems peaceful. Also, fall robins seem to perp all the time. Even though they are safely perched at the crown of the elm tree, they perp and pink as if there were a cat inches from their toenails. Long as I have known these birds, I haven't been able to figure out why they protest when they do. Perhaps, if you spend a bit of time on your porch swing, you can figure it out.

7
English Sparrows

Cheeky Foreigners on the Make

The sliding garage door behind which I park my car is a great, clumsy wall of wood, difficult to push aside under the best of circumstances. When the English sparrows have filled up the overhead track with their nests, the door becomes immovable. Each spring the sparrows and I dispute which of us shall get to use the overhead track—they for the building of their nests or I for the sliding of the door. Early on, when the weather is bad and my work schedule is heavy, I win the battle. I often park the car in the garage, and open and close the door regularly to let the car in and out. The frequent movements of the door clear the overhead track of the nest materials before they get too thick. But as spring comes on, the weather gets better and the pace of my commuting grows more languid. Now the car sits in the driveway and the garage door stands open for days at a time. Inevitably, on some grey, cold, rainy spring day, I go to put the car away and discover that the sparrows have gotten the best of me. When I try to close the door, it rolls for a bit, but then hits something as sturdy as a rock. Though I throw my shoulder against the door and push for all I am worth, all I get for my pains is a shower of straw and grass down the back of my neck. And so, each spring I eventually concede the garage to the birds.

My war with the English sparrow is part of a long-lived family tradition. My father is a birder in the grand nineteenth-century style. The moral lessons taught me at the dinner table were stern and unbending: beware pride, avarice, lechery, sloth, and the English sparrow. But above all, beware the English sparrow. Did not the English sparrow contribute to the decline of the bluebird? And does he not foul our grain supply with his litter and disturb the quiet of our winter mornings with his din? These facts were sufficient to condemn the English sparrow in my father's eyes.

One of my father's foremost concerns in life was how to feed birds in winter without feeding English sparrows. All winter long the trees in the front yard would be decorated with odd wire-mesh enclosures that dangled from their branches. Each contrivance was filled with a foul-smelling concoction of suet and birdseed that was lovingly prepared on the kitchen stove. The theory behind these arrangements was that the English sparrow had weak feet. Unlike the strong-footed nuthatches and chickadees, English sparrows couldn't hang by their toes and pull the suet and seed out through the wire mesh. Thus did my father hope to deny the English sparrow the benefits of the banquet that he regularly set for the other wintering birds.

The theatre of his summer campaign against the English sparrow was a ramshackle birdhouse that one of us children had made in a carpentry class. My father had reluctantly nailed it high up on the side of the big elm tree outside my bedroom window. The birdhouse was too shabby for fastidious birds like bluebirds or wrens, but the English sparrows loved it and they moved in early each spring. Every Saturday my father would put the ladder against the elm tree and clamber to the top, open the birdhouse, amidst the protests of the birds, and pull bushels full of packed grass and straw out of the birdhouse. Then he'd clamber down and go grumbling off to the barn with the ladder. As soon as he was around the corner of the house, the English sparrows were back, dragging the straw and hay back into the nesting box.

This ritual would continue more or less weekly until one Saturday the worst happened. I would hear from my father, teetering at the top of the ladder, a great cry of anguish.

"Cripes! They've laid an egg!" I can remember standing there at the foot of the ladder, watching my father's burly torso sway dangerously as he withdrew his hand from the nesting box. At the time, I reflected that it seemed a natural enough thing for a bird to do—to lay an egg. But to my father it seemed the epitome of the guile and ruthless criminality of the English sparrow. Of course I came to realize later that even my father, determined though he was, could not bring himself to destroy a nest once it had an egg in it. Perhaps the parents were culpable, but that egg, that tiny avian soul, deserved a chance at life without interference from him. And so each summer we never heard from him again concerning the sparrows in the nesting box.

As a child, I never could see what the fuss was all about. English sparrows seemed ordinary enough to me. Only the smart black bibs and cheek patches of the males set them apart from the other little brown birds I knew. The English sparrows seemed a cheerful, busy lot, chattering happily from the doorway of that ill-designed birdhouse outside my window. No other bird got near the house, except the swallows who hovered wistfully a few feet from the entrance while the sparrows chattered defiantly at them. I never regretted that the sparrows had won the birdhouse. I did wonder, if English sparrows were such bad birds, how they had gotten to America in the first place. To hear my father talk, the sparrows might have been delivered to the new world by the Devil himself. I imagined two blasphemously fecund English sparrows hopping forth from a golden cage with red plush appointments, a red hand with scaly fingers holding agape the door.

But the truth is much more interesting. English sparrows were brought to the United States on dozens of different occasions. People worked hard to introduce the English sparrow. Hundreds of birds were transported from England and from Germany in both large and small groups. Some were brought on the mistaken understanding that the birds would control some particular agricultural insect pest of the day, but not all. Given the diligence with which these introductions were pursued, it seems difficult to escape the inference that somebody was fond of these birds. For the English sparrow to arrive and to survive in America there must have been something about this bird that was both very special and very endearing.

In years of watching these birds and more recently of reading about them, I have begun to appreciate why people brought them to America. Unlike my father, I am not a classic nineteenth-century birder. I live on an old ramshackle farm, and what with work and keeping things up, I don't have the time or patience to choose the bird company I keep. I watch the birds that come my way, and the English sparrow has come my way in abundance. While English sparrows don't look like much—similar to the plethora of little brown birds that gather at a feeder in winter—their behavior is special. It is unlike the behavior of other birds in a variety of ways.

English sparrows are very sociable creatures. By contrast, most of the birds that occupy our gardens are territorial birds. The mated pair defends a space around its nest against all other members of the species. But English sparrows are not so jealous of their neighbors. An English sparrow defends his nest against others of his own kind, but he likes to have close neighbors. A prospecting English sparrow would sooner make his nest in a small group of English sparrows than strike out on his own. So, if you have one pair of English sparrows around your garden, the chances are that you have at least a few.

The sociability of English sparrows has to do with their pedigree. The English sparrow is a weaver finch. Weaver finches are those American birds whose huge nests you often see on television specials about African wildlife or African cultures. Thousands of weaver finches may nest in a single colony, and the birds festoon the trees with coconut-sized balls of straw and grass in which the young are raised. From this base they fan out every day to

97

forage among the grain crops, in the process doing significant damage to meager African grain supplies. When English sparrows nest in trees, they behave very much like weaver finches, although not on the same scale. A small flock of birds will decorate a tree with loose, disheveled piles of straw—as many as four or five in a small tree. The design of these nests is crude compared to an African weaverbird's nest, but the grouping of the nests is very weaverbirdlike.

For English sparrows, sociability extends to many activities. Not only do they feed together and roost together and chase predators together, they also take dust baths together. If you have a dry, dusty place in your garden, you will see little flocks of English sparrows dive into it, all chattering and excited like a bunch of kids plunging into a swimming hole. Each bird begins burrowing out a little hollow for itself in the dust. The object of this activity is to hurl as much dust as possible up onto their backs and wings. Some parts of the dust bath are better than others, and the birds squabble over who is to get the favored sites. But as fast as these little dusting parties come, they are gone again, and the birds retire in a chattering group to a nearby bush to shake themselves and preen and work the dust through their feathers.

So sociable are English sparrows that they seem often to enjoy squabbling. One night last winter we had a vigorous snowstorm that covered the ground with snow more than a foot deep. The next morning the English sparrows were loafing about as usual. I put out birdseed early in the day, and they stufed themselves and then came in a group to perch, chatter, and "just relax" on the branch of a sunny hemlock outside my study window. As they sat there, a male noticed a patch of snow on the branch of the hemlock and began pecking at it— presumably he was thirsty. Pretty soon a female came over, and she began to peck at it from the other side.

Seeing them, the rest of the flock came rushing over,
shouldering and pecking at each other to get at the snow.
To see them fuss over it, it might have been the last patch
of snow on earth.

English sparrows are very expressive birds. Among
their many behaviors is one that seems to have the same
meaning as "please." This behavior is similar to the
behavior of the young of many bird species when they beg
food from the parents. The young bird crouches, lifts its
bill, spreads and lowers its wings, and quivers them. Baby
English sparrows wing-quiver in the nest when they are
hungry, but what is remarkable is that the adults perform
versions of this same behavior in several situations that
have nothing to do with feeding. For instance, when the
young are about to fledge and the father wants them to
come out of the nest, he will perch by the side of the nest
and shiver his wings, as if to say, "Please come out of the
nest." When an adult male or female wants to mate, it will
perform a version of the shivering behavior. In this
situation, it appears to mean "Please mate with me." When
a male wants a female to try out a nest site, he will perform
the shivering behavior at the entrance of the nest hole.
Here he seems to be saying, "Please try out my nest." Thus,
among English sparrows, the behavior seems to have a
broader meaning than it does in other species. Instead of
meaning "please feed me," it means simply "please!"

Not only do English sparrows have many expressive
behaviors, they are great "talkers" as well. Most familiar
garden birds invest a lot of time and energy in singing.
Birdsong is a tuneful sound that is devoted to attracting
mates or proclaiming ownership of a territory. Since
English sparrows stay with the same mate indefinitely,
and since their territory consists only of a few cubic inches
around their nest site, they don't seem to have much use
for song. But English sparrows are almost certainly the
virtuoso chirpers of the bird world. They make every kind

99

of chirp imaginable: high-pitched chirps and low-pitched chirps; fast chirps and slow chirps; sibilant chirps and guttural chirps; sharp,staccato chirps and soft, gentle ones. They chirp when they are courting, they chirp when they are fighting, they chirp when they are taking dust baths, when they are feeding, or when they are just sitting around feeling good.

Now you might think that chirping is a poor sort of vocalization compared, say, to the artful song of a mockingbird. But do not be too hasty in your judgment. To pass such a judgment on a communication system without knowing what it means would be an error. A similar hasty judgment might be made of us humans. Compared with the hoots, coos, and whistles of many of our primate relatives, human language might seem a poor form of communication indeed, if you didn't know what it meant: a sort of muted, featureless grumbling. I suppose it's silly to think that sparrows converse, but they certainly *seem* to converse, and until we know what all their chattering means, we would be silly to think of it as mere chirping. This is another one of those puzzles that an attentive gardener might help to solve. As you go about your daily round in the garden, tune your ear to hear the variations in your sparrows' chirps. In time you may decode a language that is as complex and intriguing — if not as beautiful — as anything the mockingbird has to offer.

Because we humans have tune-loving ears, we tend to think of tuneful song as a very advanced form of sound making. But auditory prejudices may not correspond to the evolutionary facts. There is a sense in which every English sparrow chooses not to sing, but to chirp instead. Like recent fledglings of many species, fledgling English sparrows sing for a few weeks after they leave the nest. They make a sort of babbling, disorganized noise that scientists call subsong. In other species, the subsong develops into the full song characteristic of that species. But young wild English sparrows forsake their subsong in favor of chirping. Captive English sparrows can be taught to sing a respectable birdsong, if they are hand-raised as young and tutored by their human caretakers with the songs of other birds. Odd as it may seem, these fragments of evidence suggest that chirping in English sparrows is an evolutionary "advance" from the more widespread habit of the song among the sparrow's fellow songbirds.

English sparrows are homebodies. They like to live around human habitations, preferably a genteel Victorian house with lots of gingerbread ornamentation. They are very fond of the nooks and crannies in such houses and will fill them up with baskets full of dry straw. Gutters and eaves troughs are a favorite, too, as are the creeper vines that often grow on the walls of public buildings—like your local library or town hall. Farm buildings are also a favorite location for a nest, particularly if they have open windows or loose boards. A roof overhead and a good supply of winter food in view—that's what makes an English sparrow happy.

An English sparrow's attachment to his house goes way beyond that of the average bird. Most songbirds are attached to their nest for a few weeks at a time. As soon as the young have fledged, the parents renest elsewhere. More than that of any other garden bird, the nest of an English sparrow has the significance of a year-round abode. Not only do English sparrows use the nest to rear three or four broods in the summer, but after the young have gone they fuss with the nest, keeping it in good repair. Sometimes in the winter the birds will sleep in the nests, using them for shelter against the winter winds. For an English sparrow, a house is a home.

For English sparrows—which are also known as "house sparrows"—choosing a mate is all tied up with choosing a "house." In the first fall and winter of their lives, young birds, those that fledged the previous summer, can often be found wandering around in little flocks, inspecting nooks and crannies for possible nest sites. These prospecting parties are less common when the days are cold and short, more common as they become longer and warmer. But by late winter the sparrows are busy everywhere, chattering happily as they peer and poke around the eaves of dwellings and rummage through ivy on their walls. If these young prospectors have the bad manners to investigate the nest site of an adult English sparrow, they are driven off peremptorily by the angry owner.

As late winter turns into early spring, individual males break off from the prospecting parties and begin to claim particular nest sites. Each male will sit at the doorway of his newfound home and chirp. He is trying to attract the attention of passing females. If one comes by, he will chirp louder and faster and will shiver his wings like a baby bird begging for food. If she perches beside him, he will hop excitedly into his hole and hop out again, chirping vociferously. The female may then enter his nest site and inspect it. If she likes it, she will stay. From that day on, that male and female will usually be mates, as long as both continue to breed.

English sparrows are *truly* monogamous. Many familiar garden birds are said to be monogamous. What this means in most cases is that each adult has only one mate at a time and that the couple stays together over the several broods of a season. But during the winter the two members of the pair separate, and even if both survive to the next season, they rarely reunite with each other. Thus, monogamy usually means "serial monogamy." But when a pair of English sparrows mate, it is "until death do them part." Regrettably, "death does them part" fairly often. On the average, the chance that a mated pair will remain together two years running is only about one in four. Still, it is not for lack of fidelity on the part of the birds. If both survive from year to year, they will usually remain faithful to each other.

Because of their attachment to a house, English sparrows are sedentary birds. Once an English sparrow has picked out a cornice of your house to nest in, he will return day after day, month after month, season after season. Only mortality stands between him and total loyalty to your garden. About half the adult birds die in a year's time, so that if you have an English sparrow in the eaves of your house or in the ivy of the library across the street, there's a fifty percent chance that it's the same English sparrow that was there last year. And there's about a fifty percent chance that the same English sparrow will be there at this time next year.

Though it seems a paradox, the sedentary habits of the English sparrow have a lot to do with its rapid dissemination around the world. Migratory birds are navigators; they use astronomical and geological signs to find their way home. A displaced migratory bird will use the sun, the stars, and perhaps the earth's magnetic field to find its way home. English sparrows are nonmigratory. If an English sparrow gets transported several miles from its nesting place, it will just settle down where it finds itself. To an English sparrow, "home" is not a position of the stars or of the sun at noon, or a particular crinkle in the earth's magnetic field. Home is a particular building. If you take him out of sight of his home, he may not be able — or bother — to find his way back to it.

You would think that nothing would be so immovable as a bird that falls in love with houses. After all, it's a rare day when a house picks up and moves away from its foundation. But think for a moment: perhaps it's not such a rare day, after all. For an English sparrow, a house may be a houseboat, or a freighter, or a boxcar parked on a siding (particularly if the "house" is amply provided with a grain supply). If, after nesting has commenced, these conveyances are moved, the house sparrows are transported—nests, eggs, babies, and all—to a new location. Sparrows that choose the hold of an oceangoing vessel for a house may be delivered, fat and happy, to a new continent.

English sparrows are unusually sexy birds. For most familiar songbirds, mating is a perfunctory act performed only as required. Compared with the mating of such respectable birds as robins, the mating behavior of English sparrows is frequent, noisy, and public. The birds begin mating in the late winter whenever the weather is fine, and they mate often all summer long. Sparrows mate on their front porch, so to speak, at the entrance to the nest or on branches immediately nearby. Other pairs of birds in the colony often become excited when a pair mate and begin to mate themselves. It's quite a scene!

Either the male or the female of the pair may initiate a mating interaction. The initiator approaches the other bird and says "please." Its legs are bent and its wings are drawn to the side and down until the tips almost touch the surface. In this position, they are quivered delicately. A male says "please" with particular emphasis. He arches his back, puffs out his chest, elevates his rump, and rotates his wings forward to make them more visible from the front. In this pose, he struts and bows in front of his female, showing off his white rump, white wing bars, white chest, and black throat. All the time he chirps frantically. If the female is willing, she crouches and gives the wing-quivering gesture and a curious, high-pitched "tee-tee-tee" call. The male mounts and the mating is completed.

If the female is unwilling, a dramatic series of events may follow, events whose significance is a puzzle to scientists who have studied the birds. The unwilling female adopts a threat posture. She leans forward with her bill open as if to peck. Her wings are held above her body and may be flicked nervously. From this position she lunges at the male if he comes too close.

The frustrated male may now engage in a frenzy of courtship, strutting and bowing, chirping like an over-wound little mechanical soldier. The noise and flurry of the bickering couple eventually attracts the attention of the other males in the colony, who fly down to the pair to see what all the fuss is about. Once beside the female of the disputing pair, the other males may begin to court her themselves. All these bowing and strutting males are too much for the female, and she takes off to try and find a safe place to hide. After her races the group of males. The little mob of birds is in such a state of enthusiasm that they are in danger of flying into obstacles. Wherever the female perches, the males crowd around her, strutting and bowing and chirping. Soon, however, their enthusiasm wanes and they wander back to their own nests and females. The squabbling couple goes back to its nest and the whole colony quiets down again.

Scientists have only a vague idea what this excitement is all about. In many species of birds the courtship of the male serves to stimulate the female to be ready to mate and to produce eggs. Perhaps when a female is reluctant, the multiple courtship by a bunch of males is all she needs to bring her into readiness. One scientist has suggested that it is all part of a system that tends to make all females lay eggs at the same time so that breeding in the colony is synchronized. In a synchronized colony the babies would fledge at the same time, forming a natural flock. Each youngster would have the company and protection of his peers during his first few weeks of independent life.

So when you see your English sparrows rushing around your yard in a little chattering flock like so many dry leaves driven before a gust of wind, put down your hoe and take a look. You are watching another one of those many mysteries that scientists have not been able to figure out. It will give you something to think about while you're staking your peas or stretching your back after a session with the weeds among your onions.

English sparrows have lots of leisure time. Nobody would invent an adage such as "the early English sparrow gets the seed." English sparrows are among the last birds to get up in the morning and the first birds to retire in the evening. And even so, they seem to have lots of time to loaf during the day. They sit around in trees and bushes in little groups, poking at the branches or leaves or at each other in a halfhearted way and chattering contentedly.

They even like to sunbathe. One brilliant spring morning I was sitting on the south side of the house, trying to soak the winter out of my bones, when I noticed an English sparrow lolling on the roof of the garage. I thought he was dead or certainly dying. He was lying half on his side and half on his stomach, his feathers were all fluffed, his neck was bent at a strange angle, and his wings were spread limply at his side. He looked as if he had fallen from a great height and broken his neck. At any moment I expected him to fall off the sloping roof of the garage, but he didn't move at all except perhaps to shift a little, every once in a while, like somebody in a very deep sleep. Finally, my curiosity got the better of me and I stood up and clapped my hands to try and startle the bird. He leaped to his feet, so to speak, and flew off chattering indignantly. He wasn't hurt at all. He had just been taking a sunbath.

When I think of these special qualities of the English sparrow—his sociability, his garrulousness, his sexiness, his fondness for lying about in the sunshine, his homeyness and fidelity—I begin to see why it was that thousands of the birds were brought to the New World as a cure for European homesickness. Compared with other birds, there is something oddly human about these little creatures. On sunny winter days when they loll about the hemlock outside my study window, they seem like so many senior citizens taking a well-deserved rest in the sun. If they get hungry, they venture around to the other side of the house where I have scattered birdfeed on the snow. If something frightens them over there, I know immediately because the little group comes rushing back to the hemlock tree, all chattering and breathless, like a bunch of little street urchins that have played a prank on a policeman. They will sit and remonstrate in the hemlock for a few moments, and then, as their courage gathers again, they will flutter hesitantly around the corner of the house, headed for the feeding ground once more.

Fond as I am of the English sparrows, I know they have some well-deserved enemies. Farmers often dislike them, and the bird is, admittedly, an agricultural pest. Adult English sparrows are primarily granivores — they like grain. Groups of birds that gather in grain sheds in the winter foul the grain and make a nuisance of themselves. The large flocks of juveniles that collect on grainfields in the fall can also do much harm. But the dislike felt by farmers may not be entirely fair. Baby English sparrows are insectivores. Two-thirds of the food brought by the parents to the nest consists of insect larvae, many of harmful species such as the alfalfa weevil. Thus, what the birds take from the grain shed and the wheatfield in the fall and winter, they may give back in the spring by protecting crops that are in leaf.

Among the most avid enemies of the English sparrow are the partisans of the eastern bluebird. Because of its enthusiasm for nesting boxes, the English sparrow has driven the bluebird from many a house put out for it in orchards by doting bluebird lovers. Together with the starling, the English sparrow is accused of causing the decline of the eastern bluebird. The bluebird lovers argue that the English sparrow is an unnatural creature in America and that it is destroying the native ecology.

107

While I sorely miss the bluebird, I am obviously of two minds about this issue. People who argue that man has disturbed nature by bringing the English sparrow to America forget that man *is* a part of nature. Intercontinental invasions, extinctions, the rise and fall of species are all a familiar evolutionary process. It isn't unusual in nature for one species to live under the protection of another, and to spread where that species spreads. Fleas travel with dogs, lice with birds, burrs with bears, and sparrows with humans. Just because the bluebird is a handsome color and has a pretty song does not make its extermination by the English sparrow unnatural. Nothing about nature's processes require that they conform to the aesthetic tastes of human environmentalists.

But if, after all I have said, you are determined to eliminate English sparrows from your life, there is a simple but drastic measure you can take. Since the birds are sedentary and since they rely for their winter survival on food from human beings, you can probably eliminate nesting English sparrows from the vicinity of your house by not feeding birds in the winter. They will not nest in the summer where there is no winter food supply. Eliminate that winter food supply for a few winters and you will probably have no breeding English sparrows during summer.

But ridding myself of English sparrows is too much of a price to pay, even for the breathtaking beauty of a summering bluebird. While a resident bluebird would add to the pleasure of my summers, my summers are already thick with pleasure. The bluebird is a fair-weather friend. He comes to my garden when the weather is warm and the world is lush with life. But my English sparrows are foul-weather friends. Winters are long and cold and silent where I live, and not a little bit cruel. They would be longer, quieter, and crueler still without the affable chatter of the English sparrows as they sort gratefully through the food I provide them on the drift in the backyard.

8

Phoebes

Gentle
Tyrants

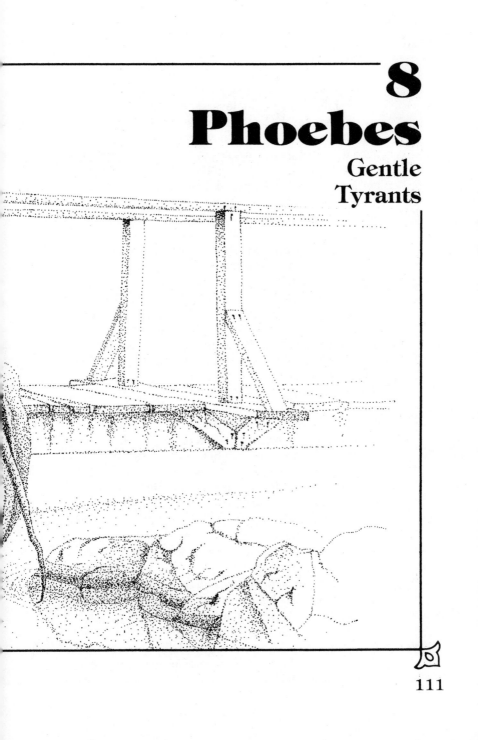

Paralyzed by spring fever, I am standing at the end of my garden. For the last ten minutes I have been trying to make a simple calculation: how many row-feet of corn do I need to plant today to ensure my family of two dozen ears during the week of July 21? The multiplication keeps getting stuck in my head and the more I struggle with it, the more remote and irrelevant the week of July 21 begins to seem. Today I have already calculated June's radishes, August's carrots, September's cantaloupe, October's cabbage, November's brussels sprouts, and next March's parsnips. For some reason, July's corn is beyond calculation.

I keep being distracted by the activity of the creatures around me. While I was planting the second-crop carrots, I was stalled twice—once to watch a woodchuck standing up tall and still like a prairie dog as he guarded his burrow in the west hayfield, and once to listen to the oriole. The oriole was rummaging through the leaves of the maple tree, singing fragments of his personal song as he foraged: "Da . . .," hop to a new branch, "di . . .," peck at something, ". . . dle . . .," hop to another new branch, ". . . diddle . . .," sashay along the branch, "dee dee," and so forth. I had never seen an oriole do that before. It seemed like I would never be able to get back to work until I heard him sing the whole theme. But I managed to wrench my mind away from the oriole and back to the garden, only to be distracted by a phoebe perched on the tiller. The tiller is parked in the entrance of the tool shed, and the neat grey little bird was parked on its handlebars, where he could supervise the comings and goings of all who might enter the shed. He must have a nest in the rafters of the shed. As often as I have been in and out of that shed in the last few weeks, I've never noticed the nest.

Seeing the phoebe reminded me of a walk I have been meaning to take for weeks to see a fellow phoebe who lives down by the river. In the region where I garden, spring comes on in a rush. There are so many things to do that I often let the season slip by. Much as I love my garden, sometimes I need to get away from it just to enjoy spring. There always comes an afternoon when the air is particularly soft and enticing, and the sun is warm on my back. On that day I have to drop my hoe in the unplanted row, put my seeds back in the seedbox, whistle up the dog, and leave the garden work to the earthworms. This afternoon is such an afternoon.

As the dog and I set out across the west field, the bobolinks come to the tops of the alfalfa stems and apprehensively watch us approaching. As we reach the boundary of each territory, its owner flutters up from his perch and circles over us. The flight is not like his normal flight, which carries him quickly and unobtrusively from place to place, but is a special showy kind of flight. The bobolink's wing beats are very rapid and elaborate, and the tips of his wings almost touch under his body at every downstroke. As he flies, the bird sings his long and effervescent song. The whole performance seems more like a greeting than like a defensive display.

At the far boundary of the west field I encounter the barbed wire fence that separates the west field from the north pasture beyond. I pause for a moment, deciding how to cross it. Without hesitating, the dog flattens himself on his belly and squirms under, so I follow his lead. I lie down on my back, lift the lowest strand of wire, and slither under. Lying here in the short grass of the pasture for a moment, I have an impulse to stay right here. Two song sparrows are matching songs from neighboring posts along the fence. They are singing the "My Country, 'Tis of Thee" theme, I think, but one of the singers is giving it a peculiar twist. It would be tempting to lie here beside the fence and try to figure out just what this new special variation is.

But I heave myself resolutely to my feet and set off down the pasture. Here the cattle have kept the grass short and I see a different group of birds. A kingbird chatters imperiously from the highest branch of an apple tree. A killdeer "tee-dees" plaintively off to my right. I see the killdeer running away with quick, mincing steps. It moves a dozen yards or so, then stops abruptly and presses itself to the ground. As soon as it stops moving, it is almost invisible, and I can make it out only by its black and white neckbands. I wonder if it is a female and if it has a nest where it is crouching. The dog apparently wonders, too; he veers from his path to investigate. Immediately the killdeer runs another dozen yards or so and then flops over on its side, flapping its upper wing spasmodically and exposing its bright yellow underfeathers. The bird books say that the killdeer is trying to convince the dog that she has a broken wing in order to lead him from her nest. But the behavior also looks a bit like the crouching and fluttering that so many birds engage in when they are trying to entice one another to feed or to mate. Is she deceiving us or is she enticing us? I cannot say.

I think it's best not to disturb her, so I call off the dog and turn aside myself. Seeing my new direction, the dog bounds across the pasture to head me off. Meadowlarks flutter away from his path, showing off the white stripes down the sides of their tails. As they settle on tufts of grass, I can hear first one, then the other sing the local meadowlark dialect. "Too late . . . too long" each seems to say. I do not know to whom they address that sad message, or even what the message means, but it adds to my determination to grasp the season while I can.

The path now dips steeply downhill through a forest of white pines. My farm is laid out on great moraines set down by the glaciers as they retreated hundreds of thousands of years ago. Since their departure, a river has been cutting down through the moraines and has made itself a narrow valley about sixty feet deep and a few hundred yards wide. Within this enclosure it wanders back and forth, forming a narrow floodplain.

The "provinces" of my farm and the agricultural uses to which they have been put have been determined by the glaciers and the river. The hayfields are on the tops of the moraines. They are great sandbanks, really, and the soil there is droughty, quick to warm in the spring and quick to dry out in the summer. The pastures and forests are on the steep sides of the moraines, where they slope down toward the floodplain. On the floor of the floodplain are a few acres of riverbottom land that was once used for corn. Since we have taken the farm over we have let it grow up to "wildlife land," and it is beginning to be quite a tangle.

So far, our walk—the dog's and mine—has carried us off the tops of the moraines, down the side of the valley, to the edge of the floodplain. Along the margin of the floodplain runs an old disused railroad track, a remnant of the thriving agricultural trade that used to characterize this region. Where the railroad crosses the river is an antique trestle bridge, rusted and covered with ivy. It is here that I intend to have my moment alone with spring. As we reach the floor of the little valley, we turn downriver on the railroad tracks. Now we begin to become aware of the birds of the riverbank. The rattling call of a kingfisher echoes over the water. A catbird mews from a dank, brushy tangle of grapevines and small trees. A wood thrush sings his liquid song from a copse of oaks and maples on the uphill side of the tracks. Through the trees I can catch glimpses of the river and see the dark forms of swallows as they hurry back and forth over its glistening surface.

When we arrive at the trestle, the dog walks out on it, cautiously placing each paw as he looks warily down between the ties. Even though we have been coming here for a long time, he and I, he still does not trust the trestle. I walk behind him, balancing on a rail so that I do not have to match my stride to the inconvenient spacing of the ties. At the middle of the bridge I step off the rail and walk out on one of the massive girders that support the railbed.

Holding on to the superstructure of the bridge, I carefully let myself down onto the end of the girder where it hangs out a dozen feet above the water. Here I can let my legs dangle down and rest my back and elbows on the wooden frame of the railbed behind me. From this vantage point I have a clear view of the water, the riverbank, and the sky. I take a deep breath.

At first my attention is drawn to the surface of the river. We have had a wet spring. The river is high and the water surges under the bridge, its surface bulging with turbulent upwellings from below. Downstream about a hundred feet, the water divides around a small island. For a time I amuse myself by watching bits of leaves and other litter carried in the flow. I try to predict on which side of the island they will pass. On the average, the dividing line seems to be just below my feet at midriver. But sometimes huge eddies form, and objects are carried swiftly from the left side of the river to pass down the right side of the island, and vice versa.

Predicting what objects will end up where turns out to be a more interesting game than I had supposed it would be, and I devote several minutes to it.

But then my attention is drawn to the birds flying under the bridge. A spotted sandpiper has been fluttering up and down the river. I used to think that this species was a coastal bird, but the field guides have often assured me that I may find him here. In a few weeks, when the weather is drier and the river is lower, I will see him tippy-toeing and poking his way across the little mud flats at the river's edge. A kingfisher swooped through the bridge once, so rapidly that I caught only a glimpse of his brilliant blue plumage. And, of course, I have seen dozens of swallows. As they pass beneath me I can recognize the different kinds much more easily than when I see them silhouetted against the sky: the barn swallows with their deeply forked tails, the cliff swallows with their bright beige rumps, the tree swallows with their metallic green backs, and the dull brown bank swallows. Like the river itself, the swallows seem to flow through the bridge in irregular swirls and eddies.

But delighted as I am to see the water birds, I really have come to see a particular phoebe, a little troll of a bird who lives under this bridge and every year comes fearlessly to greet me whenever I visit here. I have some of the same feelings toward this creature that I would have to a confidant whom I had met casually in some beautiful park year after year and told my troubles to. The longer I sit here on the bridge without seeing him, the more I worry about him. Perhaps he was waylaid on his migration from the Gulf Coast states. It is such a long way to travel for such a small bird.

But as soon as I make a determined effort to find my friend, I locate him high up on the edge of the vertical palisade of brush and vines that walls the river in. He is perched out on the end of a twig, hunting insects. Every so often he flutters out into space, twisting, turning, gyrating, until he seems to seize something in his beak. Then he flutters back to the perch. Here he whacks the something he has caught on the twig a few times to soften it up, swallows it with some difficulty, shakes himself, and then looks around him. He seems almost a bit embarrassed, like a restaurant diner who has taken an improperly large mouthful. Did anyone else notice?

The crisp motions of the phoebe, his erect bearing, and his elegant grey and white plumage remind me that he is a tyrant. The phoebe is a member of a family of birds known as the tyrant flycatchers. They get their name from one of the largest of their number, the kingbird, whose Latin name is *Tyrannus*. The kingbird looks a bit like a large phoebe, being basically dark grey above and light grey below, but his plumage is very elegant. Like the phoebe, the kingbird is an insect hawk who mostly makes his living snatching insects out of the air or pouncing on them in the grass. As a consequence of this habit, his perching posture is very erect and very regal. In addition, he has an inconspicuous red spot on the top of his head—a crown, if you will—and a dressy white fringe on the ends of his tailfeathers, sort of a white ermine fringe on the skirt of his grey royal robe. Despite his regal plumage, the kingbird probably gets his Latin name from his temperament. He is the most aggressive of birds. The kingbird will attack any bird, no matter how large, that has the bad manners to wander near his nest tree.

Perched on the end of his twig, my phoebe does not seem in a tyrannical frame of mind. He looks to the right, then to the left, then leans forward and deftly snatches a gnat out of the air. He then takes off and darts upstream, passing overhead and beyond the bridge. I lose sight of him for a moment, but almost immediately hear his song, "Phoebee! Phoebee! Phoebee!" he says insistently. It is a matter-of-fact sound, the song of the phoebe, like a routine announcement, a mundane assertion made without fear of contradiction.

But despite my pleasure at hearing the phoebe's song, it makes me worry a bit for the little bird. He should not be singing so much. During the day a male usually sings for long periods only when he is establishing a territory and looking for a mate. Otherwise, his singing is mostly confined to the early-morning hours. This late in the spring, a male phoebe should have his territory well established. He should be comfortably mated, his nest should be built, and his mate should be incubating the eggs. Could it be that my phoebe has been unable to find a mate? Or could it be that he found a mate but she was lost to a predator? Nest destruction is not a frequent occurrence for phoebes, since they nest securely under overhangs and over water, but still it is possible that a marauding sparrow hawk or chipmunk may have found the nest.

By now the phoebe's calling has become more irregular. The tempo and cadence seem constantly to change. Sometimes it is "pheebee," sometimes "pheeblee." Sometimes the sounds seem to crowd together, sometimes they are well spaced. When the sounds come quickly and they vary, the bird seems upset.

Why is it that I so often feel that I can guess what a bird is feeling from its sounds? Many birds' songs have meanings to me. The meadowlark's song arouses sadness in me, the song sparrow's song suggests patriotism. The bobolink's makes me feel welcome; the song of the thrush, lonesome. The chickadee's song seems friendly to me, whereas the thrasher's song seems unfriendly. Of what value are these intuitions? Surely these birds' songs cannot be designed for the effects they produce in me. Of what use is it to a meadowlark to make a forty-five-year-old gardener feel sad, or to a chickadee to make him feel befriended? Somehow these "meanings" seem to say more about me than they do about the birds. Does my intuition that the phoebe has become agitated have any value? Do the changes in his song "mean" that he is upset?

What is meaning to a bird? When I think about meaning I always think about the meaning of words. The word "tomato" stands for the red fruit of the tomato plant. When I say "tomato," I am using the word to name the fruit. Birds' songs obviously do not have meaning in this way. When a bird sings, he does not name his territory, or name the mate he hopes to attract, or competitors he hopes to exclude. Birds' songs must "mean" in a way that is different from the way in which words "mean."

Perhaps there is another sense of meaning that may be more helpful to our understanding of what birds' songs mean. Let us imagine that my wife has just asked me, for

119

the third time today, if I would take the "garden garbage" out to the compost heap. And let us say that upon hearing this request, I sigh deeply. I may not have even been aware of this sigh, but it is brought sharply to my attention when my wife asks me what I *mean* by it.

With my sigh and her question we have entered into a new domain of meaning. It is difficult to point to anything that the sigh "means." It certainly does not refer to the garbage or to the compost heap. But if we asked my wife what the sigh meant, she would have no difficulty in replying. She would say quickly that the sigh meant that I was ill-disposed to take out the garbage and that I was likely to become testy if she pressed the matter. Her observations have the ring of truth. Is this, then, the meaning of my sigh? Did the sigh refer to things that I would do? Did it refer to my disposition?

If so, we now have an understanding of meaning that makes it possible to discover what birdsong means to a bird. The meaning of a song is what it reveals about the disposition of the singer. To interpret the phoebe's song, we need to surmise what it tells us about the likely future behavior of the phoebe. If we can surmise that the bird will attack a male phoebe who enters his territory, or court a female, then these reasonable surmises constitute the meaning of the phoebe's song.

When you start thinking about birds' sounds in this way, you realize that some of their sounds really do mean what they seem to mean. A fledgling crow seized on the ground makes agonized squeals that cause the adult crows to approach and dive on the fledgling's captor. As they approach they make sounds that seem angry. And everything about the crows' behavior suggests that these sounds mean what they seem to me to mean: that the baby's sound means that it is calling for help and trying to escape, and that the adults' sounds mean that they intend to attack. Why should our intuitions about the meaning of birds' sounds sometimes be correct and sometimes turn out to be mere anthropomorphism?

The fact is that there appear to be some very general rules about animal sounds that apply equally to birds and to humans. The rules suggest that increases in speed and loudness of a sound often denote increases in the animal's disposition to act. They suggest that low, vibrant sounds like growls and rattles are often signs of aggressive intent, while high-pitched sounds often give evidence of intention to flee. Whenever a bird's sounds go along with one of these general rules, then our intuitions about the meaning of the sounds may be quite useful. But, of course, when the sounds do not correspond to one of these general rules, the feelings that the sound evokes in human listeners give no evidence of its real meaning.

I am jolted out of my reverie by the sight of a second phoebe. At first I think it is a female answering my phoebe's call, but as soon as my phoebe flies over, the visitor flies away upriver and disappears into some briars. It must be a prospecting male, although it is very unusual for male phoebes to intrude on one another during the nesting season. The territories are well scattered, and breeding male phoebes do not normally have close neighbors to come into conflict with. If it was a prospecting male, his intrusion explains why my phoebe is singing during the day. The single exception to the general rule that mated phoebes do not sing during the day is the rare case in which an intruding male enters the territory. On such occasions the territorial male will revert to behavior more typical of early season, and begin to sing. Perhaps my phoebe's nest mate has not been lost, after all.

Having dispatched the intruder on his way, the resident male phoebe returns downriver to perch once again in the wall of brush where I first saw him. He seems more at ease now. He flicks his tail and wings less often.

121

He even takes off for a moment to snatch a passing insect out of the air. I resolve to settle the question of whether he has an active nest. Navigating very carefully, I let myself gently down among the underpinnings of the bridge. It is dark under there and it takes several moments for my eyes to adjust. I carefully inspect each of the members of the bridge, looking for a tuft of mud and grass that might be a phoebe nest. In time I find such a nest tucked away on one of the supports of the bridge. Sitting in it, silhouetted against the bright sunlight on the other side of the bridge, is a female phoebe. All is well down by the river this spring!

Once on my feet, I realize that it is time to get back to my gardening. The weekend is almost over and I still do not have all the corn in. Another week's delay and I will not have a chance of getting any July corn. I scramble back onto the trestle and retrace my steps down the track. Up the patch through pinewoods and into the north pasture I climb, the dog following along behind me reluctantly.

As we come through the north pasture, the meadow-larks and the song sparrows are quiet, but the kingbird sits imperiously on his perch. As we pass beneath his observation tree, he almost seems to scowl down on us. The dog and I slither under the fence together, he just ahead of me. As I inch my way under, he takes advantage of the moment of my vulnerability to give my face a good lick. I shout at him, and he bounds off, tail and ears high, step light, while I dry my face with the back of a sleeve. It is an old game between us and he has fairly won that round.

Back at the garden, the dog goes off to find his water bowl and I return to my rows of corn. I pick up my hoe and the seed packet of early corn. Let me see now, at 1½ ears per foot, how many row-feet will I need in the week of July 21? Three dozen ears sounds good. So I confidently measure out three eight-foot-long furrows with the hoe and begin to drop the seeds into the earth.

9
Red-Winged Blackbirds
Pushy Polygamists

"WILL SUMMER NEVER COME ?!" I am tempted to yell and shake my fist at the sky, but it would do no good. The clouds are so low that they sever the tops of local hills and make the familiar landscape seem alien. Overhead, the indistinct grey sky seems to rest on the tops of the trees that ring my garden. In the garden, the maximum/minimum thermometer tells a dismal tale: the high temperature yesterday was 54 degrees. The low last night was 51 degrees. The plastic sheets that I draped over my early tomatoes, peppers, and eggplants in the hope of collecting some heat now collect only moisture. Puddles accumulate in hollows in the plastic, and the sheets weigh heavily on the tender plants. I lift up a corner of the plastic. There is no sign of growth, and the plants look flattened and bruised. Something has been eating at the eggplants, and they look more like deer's antlers than like the bushy little plants I put out a week ago.

Saddest of all is the corn. In the first week of May we had a hot spell so vigorous that I thought the cold could never return. So I planted corn down at the end of the garden, beyond the peas. The heat conjured the corn out of the ground. In a few days the plants' delicate green rolls fractured the crusty soil surface like an earthquake. But then the cold snap came. A cold grey mist rolled in from the North Atlantic and the corn stopped growing. Worst of all, something or somebody started pulling up the plants. Here and there the tiny rolls are strewn along the row. The bloated kernels attached to the roots of the small plants have been punctured and robbed of their substance. Damn! Only a day or two more of good growth and the plants would have been safe. Their roots would have been too strong to pull up, and too much of the substance of the kernel would have been used to make the pulling worth the effort. But as it is, the seedlings are helpless against the predator, whoever it may be. I will probably have to replant the entire row.

Disconsolately I start back toward the house. The water from the drenched grass has begun to seep through my shoes and my feet are wet. As I pass the row of Normandy poplars planted along the side of the barn, a bird begins clucking at me self-importantly from the top of one of the trees. I stop in the driveway and we eye one another. "Honkaree," the bird sings, fluffing out brilliant scarlet shoulder patches. It's a red-winged blackbird. With its song, it claims territorial rights over my garden. With its clucking call, it declares that I am an intruder. The bird opens its wings and sails down to the top of one of the pea stakes. "Honkaree!" it repeats, and drops down among my corn rows.

I pick up a few rocks from the driveway and skulk back toward the end of the garden. As I come around the pea trellises I catch the blackbird in the act of destroying my corn. It has one of my little corn plants pinned beneath a claw and it pecks viciously at the kernel. I hurl one of my stones, but it misses widely. The bird flies back to the poplar. "Honkaree," it says, "Belongs to meee!" I hurl the remaining stones at the poplar tree. One hits the tree and filters harmlessly through its leaves. The other sails through the foliage and thuds against the clapboard side of the barn, narrowly missing a window. The bird clucks indignantly from within the safety of the tree. For another moment we stare at each other. Then I admit defeat and trudge back toward the house. I can't be out here throwing stones all day. So what if I have to replant the corn. I'll just have to choke back my organic pride and use crow repellent on the seed. The later corn will probably catch up. And I can't be bothered with a jurisdictional dispute with a dumb bird.

"Honkaree!" the bird says, as I turn the corner of the garage. "Belongs to meee!"

I shouldn't be angry at this redwing. He's probably

127

not much keener to have a territory that includes my garden than I am to have him there. His territory is a great, diffuse no-bird's-land that extends from my garden down to the edge of the marsh a few hundred feet away. My garden may be a preferred property for song sparrows and robins and for me, but to a red-winged blackbird, living here is a sort of banishment. My redwing would prefer to be down at the center of the marsh where the cattails grow. There a small territory would provide him and his offspring with a rich food supply. There the females would crowd around him, bickering to see who would have the right to share his territory and raise his young.

You see, male red-winged blackbirds are polygamists— at least, the fortunate ones are. A few of my male redwings have several mates, while some have only one mate, and a great many don't have any mates at all. To understand why there is such variety in the family habits of male red-winged blackbirds, we have to look at my marsh the way a female redwing looks at it. For nesting purposes, the most desirable part of the marsh is the center, where water stands much of the year and no trees or bushes can grow. Here rank grasses cover the soil and the earth is damp and rife with organic matter all summer long. Such a habitat is a veritable larder of the insects that baby blackbirds need to eat in order to grow.

The next most desirable part of my marsh is the hummocky ground just above the cattails. In damp years this land is as good for the raising of young blackbirds as the cattail marsh. In dry years it becomes dusty and hard, and the females have difficulty finding food for all of their babies. Of course in April and May, when the females are starting to build their nests, there's little way for them to know what sort of a season—wet or dry—the summer will be. So the female who nests in the hummocky ground above the cattails runs more risks than a female who builds her nest in the cattails.

Least desirable of all are the upland pastures and woods (and gardens!) that surround the marsh. Food is less plentiful here, and a female redwing who tries to raise a brood in the uplands has to travel farther to forage for her young. Without the thick, hard spears of cattails or reeds to camouflage her nest from above and the water to protect it from below, her nest is vulnerable to airborne and terrestrial marauders alike, such as the crows and jays. No female blackbird who had a choice would voluntarily start her nest in such unblackbirdy surroundings. Thus, the male redwing with whom I have been bickering is probably as disappointed in love as I am in gardening.

The complex social order that banished my male redwing to my garden has taken weeks to develop. When the males return north in the spring, they head for the cattail march. The competition for territories is very intense. Males flutter in from cattail to cattail, ruffling out their scarlet shoulder patches and fanning out their black tails and giving the "honkaree" call. If another male comes too close, the bird claiming the territory may fly at it, clucking vigorously, and may even attack it. If a bird is to maintain a territory in the cattail marsh, he must be alert, strong, and tireless. Constantly harassed by other males, he must eat "on the wing," as it were. Only the strongest, healthiest, and most experienced birds can take the strain of this sort of competition, and even they must content themselves with maintaining small territories.

Many of the male redwings cannot find space for even a small territory in the cattail marsh. Some of these disenfranchised males stake out territories in the hummocky ground around the marsh. Here the competition is less intense and the territories are larger. If still more males are left over, these remaining birds will stake out territories in the peripheral upland around the hummocky ground. So few birds contest this undesirable ground that the territories here are very large.

After the males are settled, the females begin to stake out their claims in the cattail marsh. With little regard to which male holds which territory, the females attempt to claim their own little bit of marsh against the claims of other females. You would think that a female redwing, being almost as big as the male and having a bill nearly as long and as sharp, could defend a territory as large as the male, but she can't. Unlike males, who usually seem to have no responsibilities but to defend their territories, females have to build nests, lay eggs, incubate the young, and all the while feed themselves well enough to make energy available for all these activities. Because the resources of the cattail marsh are rich enough to support several broods of blackbirds on a single male's territory, the females do best who devote only a little time to chasing off other females and devote most of their time to getting down to the business of building a nest and laying eggs in it.

So, when a prospecting female finds one or more females already on a male's territory, she has a choice to make. She can try to nest on that male's territory and resist the competitive efforts of the other females. Or she can move out to the hummocky ground where she might find a male with a territory not already occupied by a female. Which choice makes the most sense for her depends on how many other females are already on the territory, how much food is available there, and how far along in the breeding cycle the other females are. If the new female is willing to wait to begin her breeding until the other females are too distracted with nesting and brooding to vigorously defend their territories, in the long run the newcomer will be assured some space in the territory. But she is taking a big chance. Her brood will be delayed. Late broods of blackbirds are more likely to fail or be attacked by predators, and if they do fail, there is no time to start them over.

Under these circumstances, it might pay the female to leave the center of the marsh and choose a place to nest in the hummocky ground, or even in the uplands, where conditions are not so luxurious but where she can begin her breeding immediately, and without the interference of other females. Thus it is that the polygamous social order of the red-winged blackbirds takes shape in my marsh during the course of the spring. If we went exploring together in the marsh, you and I, we would find at its center a number of males with small territories containing several females. At the edges of the marsh we would find fewer males, with somewhat larger territories, containing fewer females. Beyond, in the upland woods and pastures, we would find a few males with very large territories, containing only one or perhaps no females at all.

If you asked the redwings from the marsh what they thought of the ground around my garden, they would probably say it was fit for a meadowlark or a robin or a bobolink, but certainly no good for a redwing. Only the poor redwings live out here. And so the poor redwings do, biding their time, hoping for a calamity to befall one of the residents of the prime territories in the cattail marsh. Patiently they wait, growing older, learning skills of territorial conquest, getting to know the hazards and resources of the area, awaiting the day when there will be a space for them in the marsh. Had I been in a reflective mood the day I found my ruined corn, I might have realized that it was just such a marginal blackbird that was trying to console himself in his ecological disappointment by eating my corn.

Blackbird society is fascinating to watch. Sometimes, when the summer air is light and cool, the sun is bright and the bugs aren't too bad, I can hear the birds calling from the marsh, and I like to put down my hoe, climb over the pasture fence, and stroll down the path to a large, flat rock overlooking the marsh. When I get to the rock, I

131

climb up on top of it and loll on its flat top, watching the birds as they go about their busy, complicated social lives.

If you are a person who enjoys complicated social situations, you also might enjoy taking a few hours off from your busy gardening schedule some afternoon and going down to watch the redwings in your blackbird marsh. Don't forget to take your binoculars. They really help you to see what's going on without intruding on it. As you approach the marsh, the birds will fly up to the tops of the trees, bushes, or clumps of cattails and make clucking noises. They are warning one another of your approach. Find yourself a comfortable place where you can relax without shifting or fidgeting. You will want to pick your spot carefully, because there are many insects in a blackbird marsh—mosquitoes and blackflies, for instance— and it will be hard to sit still while you are being eaten alive. Pick out a dry place that's a little elevated—the limb of a tree; a fallen log; a boulder or stone wall; even a dry, sunny slope—and the bugs will have a harder time finding you. If you brought your dog with you, you'll have to call it to your side and get it to lie down; otherwise, the only thing you will see is fluttering male redwings and the only thing you'll hear is clucking sounds. Be patient. Be prepared to sit for ten minutes or so. Often after a disturbance the birds lay low, as if they are suspicious or making up for lost feeding time.

If you stay put, the birds will eventually go back to their normal activities, the raising of young and the defense of territories. At first you will have difficulty seeing any pattern in what is going on, but gradually a pattern will emerge. Start by paying attention to the adult males. Look for them by listening for their honkaree calls. If they are in sight, you will recognize them by their deep black color and brilliant red shoulder patches. When a male is feeding or just flying about, the patches may be a bit hard to see, but when he has his territorial dander up, he ruffles out his feathers and the red patches suddenly blossom on his shoulders. Once you get a particular male in sight, try to keep him in sight. Train your binoculars on him and stay with him as long as possible. If he's a typical male blackbird, he will spend most of his time perched on the tops of bushes or cattails in the marsh or in the tops of trees at the edge of the marsh. From this vantage point he will survey his territory, looking this way and that and occasionally singing his honkaree song. Every once in a while he will fly away from his perch and sail across the marsh to land on another perch. During these flights he'll show his shoulder patches and make himself look big and threatening. If you follow an individual bird around with your eyes, you will find that he returns again and again to the same perches. Draw a dotted line in your mind from perch to perch, so that the several perches used by your bird form the points on a polygon. The area inside this polygon is approximately your blackbird's territory.

Now fix your eye on another nearby male redwing. It doesn't matter which one, just so long as it's not the same one you have been watching. Follow this bird with your eyes or binoculars as carefully as you did the first one. It, too, will spend a lot of time moving from perch to perch, showing its shoulder patches, and giving its honkaree call. As casual as these movements may seem at first, they, too, after a while will mark out a part of the marsh that is the second bird's territory. If you keep up this procedure for an hour or so with different birds, you will eventually have the whole marsh mapped out in your mind into the territories of its male red-winged blackbirds.

The relationships among the territories are interesting. The territories of the different birds will overlap very little if at all. Each bird pretty much keeps to his own territory and keeps out of the territories of the others. If two birds use the same perching place, they will usually do so at different times. For instance, if there is a bush in front of you that is on the boundary between two territories, one to the left and one to the right, you may see both the left bird and the right bird in this bush from time to time, but not usually at the *same* time. If the right bird is using the bush, the left bird will be off at another perch on the other side of his territory. If the left bird is using the perch, the right bird will be on the other side of his territory. If the two birds ever do end up in the same bush, there may be a scuffle, with the two birds flying about each other and giving lots of honkaree calls.

Once you have the territories marked out in your mind, concentrate your attention within one of them. After a time, you will begin to notice the comings and goings of dark brown birds that are just about the same size as or a little smaller than the adult male redwings. These are the females. They are harder to follow, mostly because they fly only little short flights or dart in and out among the reeds and grass. If an unprotected female wanders through the marsh, the resident males will pursue her, each male taking up the pursuit in turn as the female passes over his territory. Sometimes the female will drop to the ground in the male's territory, and the male will perch over her giving the honkaree call, claiming her for his own.

If you spend much time watching the blackbirds in your marsh, you will become aware of how much division of labor there is between the two sexes during the breeding season. A female does all of the nest building, all of the egg laying and incubating, and all of the feeding of the young. All the male does is defend the territory against other males and predators. On the whole the male redwing seems a lazy and indulgent sort of fellow, but during an attack by a hawk on the marsh he earns his keep.

If you are sitting by a marsh when a hawk intrudes, you know something is up. First, you will hear dozens of "fseee" calls—sharp, high-pitched whistles with a hissing

quality to them. Look around, and on every side you will
see male redwings sitting on the tops of things — tops of
bushes, tops of cattails and bulrushes, tops of trees. Look
up and you will probably see the hawk circling over the
marsh. Now the action begins.

As the predator passes overhead, one or two of the
redwings may give chase. In these aerial battles the
blackbird displays great courage and persistence. A male
redwing uses his greater maneuverability to stay above
the predator in order to dive on it and peck at it. The large
predatory birds don't like this treatment and flee as best
they can. Crows usually fly off into the woods, but a hawk
may elect to make his escape by climbing. Now the
blackbird is faced with a truly difficult predicament. As
the hawk swings around in lazy circles over the marsh, the
hot air currents carry it upward. At risk for its life, the
blackbird must stay above the hawk. It flaps its wings
vigorously to do so. At each turn of the spiral the hawk
rises higher, and so must the blackbird. The climb
continues with the blackbird still flapping and diving on
the back of the hawk. At each dive the hawk loses its
concentration and loses a bit of altitude, but immediately
it swings around and resumes its climb. The blackbird
scrambles to regain its altitude advantage and to prepare
another dive. Together, they spiral upward, higher and
higher, until the blackbird seems no more than a speck
against the sky. But the game must soon end. The higher
they go, the greater is the risk to the blackbird and less is
the threat the hawk poses to the marsh. Yet the blackbird
dares not break off the chase, for to do so would place him
lower than the hawk. Up they go, until finally the male
redwing peels off and flies as rapidly as he can to the
shelter of his marsh.

On your way back from your visit to the redwing
marsh, you may see one or more redwing cousins.
Meadowlarks nest in the upland pastures around the marsh.

You'll know them by their plaintive whistled song. Orioles nest in the tall elms that fringe the pasture. They build their socklike nests in the foliage of the elm branches.

But of all the blackbird cousins, I think the bobolink is my favorite. The bobolink is similar to the blackbird in almost every way. The male is brightly colored—yellow, black, and white—and the female is nondescript. Their social customs are similar. Like the redwing, the species is polygamous and each male has several females. The females on a territory mate in turn, reeling off brood after brood as the brief breeding season passes by. The two species have a similar repertoire of calls: the little "chuck" and "check" noises of the two species are so similar that often I get them confused along the hedgerow that separates my marsh from my hayfields.

But there is one remarkable difference. Redwings don't make much of their song. The males sail languidly from song post to song post in their territory, giving their hoarse, economical honkaree, a poor excuse for a song by any reasonable standard. In contrast, the bobolink charges into the air with a lilting, bubbling shout of song. He flutters high over his territory in a great circle, each undulation in his fluttering flight seeming to emphasize the bubblings and eddyings of his extraordinary song. Finally, he holds his wings in an arc below his body, as if cupping the air between them, and glides back to his perch.

Not only is the song flight of the bobolink an amazing performance, the song itself is an intricate bit of artwork. The birds of a meadow are like a whole guild of skilled craftsmen. Their songs are assembled from a shared collection of several dozen notes in common, which each bird may use to compose a song. The notes are strung together into short tunes, which in turn are woven together to make the whole song. Like musicians who all know the old favorites, the birds of a meadow can all sing the tunes of that meadow. But a male bobolink is an artist and he has tastes and preferences. Each bird has his favorite tunes, which he sings more frequently than the others. And all birds improvise on the tunes, adding notes to the end of a tune before going on to the next. The song is so rapid that it's hard to hear tunes, let alone the individual notes. But you will notice, as you cross a bobolink field, that as each male rises up to defend his territory against you, the song he gives is similar to—but just a little different from—the songs of the others. Each new male you encounter is like a composer who has created variations on a commonly shared theme.

It may be the early robin that gets the worm, but it's the late farmer that has the bobolinks. On my farm the bobolinks favor the best part of the hayfield where the alfalfa tufts stick up above the tops of the grasses. If my farmer were prompt, he would take the hay in early June when the greenery is succulent and protein-rich. But June is when the bobolinks are just finishing up their broods, and the mowing and raking and baling would devastate their nursery. Fortunately, the man who makes my hay is a late farmer and he cuts the hay just a few days before the Fourth of July. I guess it's a good thing, because as I look around at the farms in my neighborhood, I notice that early farmers have no bobolinks. Even my late farmer takes his toll. Though the bobolink breeding season is about over when my farmer comes to do my fields, still there are always a few stragglers trying to raise a late brood. As the mowing machines plod back and forth across the field, the birds fly up and perform their beautiful song flights in the vain hope of scaring off the big machines. It's a sad sight.

I have considered not having my fields mowed at all so that the bobolinks can continue their breeding as long as they want to. But there is an odd paradox. Around here, anyway, bobolinks breed only where the ground is mowed. They don't breed in the marshland where the blackbirds breed, and they won't use the pastures where the meadowlarks raise their young. So it seems that even though the mowing cruelly concludes the breeding of the bobolinks each year, something about it makes the ground suitable for bobolinks. Unless the field is regularly mowed, the bobolinks won't return to breed in it.

It is an odd silence that grips the farm the day after the hay is cut. The brightly colored males no longer dance over the hayfield. Their bubbling song is stilled. The crows riffle through the windrows of hay, looking for food for their clamoring young. The first broods of starlings, already flocking like they do in September, waddle in the stubble looking for insects on the exposed soil surface. The swallows dip and wheel over the tractor as the farmer prepares the hay for baling. From the cattail marsh comes the hoarse repetitive honkaree of the male redwings, as they patrol the boundaries of their territories.

10
Crows
Complex Societies of the Bird World

It is a hazy, hot June afternoon. I am planting the last of the summer crops: melons, squash, and a few rows of very late corn. On purpose, I have saved the gardening for the hottest part of the afternoon. Even though weeks have passed since the last frost, I am still trying to bake winter out of my bones. I started by turning the soil with the tiller, and now as I work my way down the corn row, dropping the seed, my bare feet sink deep in the velvety soil. When I kneel in the row to adjust a misplaced seed I am sheltered from the wind, and I can feel the sun's heat building up on my back. I'm getting a terrible sunburn, but never mind. It feels good to be warm.

At the end of the last corn row, I drop the remaining handful of seeds in the row and stand to survey the garden. With the completion of this row, the garden is now at its largest extent. Of course there will be more planting later in the season. The last of the spinach will give way to late beans. The early beans will give way to the late broccoli. But there never will be more square feet under cultivation than there are now. The planting season ebbs from here.

All afternoon while I have tilled and planted, a pair of crows have been foraging in the large hayfield to the west of my garden. I have seen them to-ing and fro-ing to the evergreen copse north of the garden where they have a nest. On the nestbound, northward trip they have the wind behind them and fly quickly. It is a direct, vigorous flight, and their wings are flicked forward crisply on each stroke. The birds remind me of skilled oarsmen hurrying across still water in small dories. But on the return southward trip the wind buffets them and they sail and plunge in its currents. It is hard work, this lugging of food to their youngsters, but they have kept at it, steadily, purposefully, all afternoon long.

About 4 P.M. the milky sky begins to turn grey in the west and the wind slacks off suddenly. For the last half hour I have been smoothing the seedbed with the back of a rake—more an aesthetic than an agricultural exercise, since the tough little corn plants grow quickly in this hot soil and won't care much if the ground is level about their feet. Moreover, the clouds building in the west suggest that nature intends to do some of her own landscaping, so I leave off mine and begin to put away my tools. With the sun behind clouds and the wind quiet, the air is soft and tropical, so mild I can barely feel it.

At this moment, life seems incomparably good. Even the balky tiller starts on the first pull of the rope, and it putters contentedly as we stroll together back to the tool shed. Returning to the garden, I bring a sledgehammer and give each of the pea poles a whack to steady them in case we have a squall. Nothing else remains to be done. The tomato plants are too small to suffer much wind damage. The mature spinach leaves look fat and brittle, but hail is rare around here and there's not much to be done about it, anyway. So, I resolve to put the sledge away and find a nice spot to lie about, to watch my crows and to wait for the storm to come on. After taking back the sledgehammer, I grab the extra pair of binoculars I always keep handy on a nail in the tool shed, and I'm off to do a bit of birding.

About a hundred yards north of my garden is a tiny low knoll, barely twenty feet around and only ten to twenty feet above the surrounding terrain. It is one of the many mounds and hollows that were sculpted by the glaciers when they rumbled through my farm hundreds of thousands of years ago. Moss and fine grass grow over its top, and the ground is as soft as a goosedown quilt. This knoll is one of many places on the farm I use for thinking.

As luck would have it, the knoll almost looks down on the small copse of evergreens where the crows have their nest. Busy with my garden all spring, I have not had time to search out the nest. Even though I know roughly where it is, it will be no small trick to find it. Crows are very secretive when they are breeding. Their approach to their nest is extremely cautious and circumspect. They never come to the nest directly, but fly first to a prominent perch in a nearby tree from which they carefully survey the countryside before making their final approach. Only then will they slip quietly through the foliage to the nest, artfully positioning themselves behind the trunks of trees if they think they are being watched.

As I settle down at my knoll, I see one of the crows drop down from the top of a large white pine and fly southward low and fast through the tops of smaller trees and out onto the west field. I study the white pine from which the crow took off. An old tree with massive black branches and relatively thin foliage, it is the sort of tree I would expect the crows to nest in. But more likely this is their "watch" tree, the tree where they pause as they fly to and from the nest. A few minutes later this guess is confirmed. The second crow returns from the west field and lands in the top of the pine. Here it perches for several minutes, looking about and flicking its tail. Even though I am a hundred yards distant, I am sure he has seen me and is deciding whether to run the risk of going to the nest. I sit very still. A grumble of thunder comes from over the low hills to the west. Not moving my head, I look up from the white pine at the threatening sky. When I look back the crow is gone.

Suddenly I hear from down the slope behind the evergreen plaintive cries, almost like the bleating of very small lambs.

"Aaar . . . aar . . . . . aar . . . . aar . . . ."

It is the begging calls of the young crows. I scan with the binoculars the tops of the trees around the watch tree, but I can't see any signs of a nest. From the slow pace of the babies' calls I know that the parent bird has not yet come to the nest. It is perched nearby where the young can see it. A moment later the calls increase in pace and pitch.

"AAR...AAR...AAR..AAULP!ULP!ULP!.."

This is the sound the babies make as food is actually shoved down their throats. Again I strain my eyes to find the nest, but I can see no trace of it.

The parent crow reappears at the top of the pine, flicking its tail nervously. The thunder grumbles again, more insistently this time. In a moment the crow is off its perch and headed south again, flying swiftly in the quiet air. The sky flickers and a louder peal of thunder rolls and rumbles up and down the valley. I ought to take shelter, but I am determined to find that nest.

What puzzles me most is that the sounds appear to come directly from the watch tree. It would be very unusual for a crow to fly directly to and from its nest tree, but my senses insist that this is the case. I train the battered binoculars on the tree and move over its trunk and branches from bottom to top. Nothing! I start down the tree again, and suddenly a movement catches my eye. I study the image. Most of the field of the binoculars is taken with the bare scaffold of the watch tree. No nest here, yet there is some motion in the unfocused background. I rock the focus bar on my binoculars. Suddenly I am looking at a young crow standing on the edge of a nest. I have had an extraordinary stroke of good luck. I am looking through the open branches of the watch tree to the top of an oak behind it. Balanced in the crown of the oak is a platform of sticks with four young crows in it. Two of them are boldly standing on the edge of the nest. From time to time they flap their wings and strain their legs and necks impatiently. Two other babies huddle in the cup of the nest.

The thunder sounds again, and both I and the birds are pelted with large, sparse raindrops. The youngsters flinch and shake their heads. The two bold ones retreat from the edge of the nest and snuggle down next to their siblings. A veil of rain shrouds the west wall of my valley, barely a mile away. Suddenly there is a vigorous flash of lightning, followed by thunder as brittle and quick as the snapping of a whip. I make a run for it.

Safely indoors, I stare at the rain pelting down on my garden and think about my crows. Crows like an open space to feed in and a tall sturdy tree to nest in, so they are fondest of nesting in places where meadows and forests are interspersed. But crows will nest in many places that don't have these amenities, and many more gardeners have crows in their gardens than know it. Even the closely packed suburbs of cities like Boston or Philadelphia or New York, the crows visit people's lawns and gardens in the early-morning hours of the long summer days, before the owners are stirring. But if you are fortunate enough to have a large meadow near your garden, you will surely have nesting crows nearby, and you can gauge the progress of their family life by counting the number of crows you see in your meadow.

In early spring, when the grass is just beginning to green, you will usually see two crows in your field, wandering about and pecking at the moist ground. These are the birds that "own" your field. They are your neighbors. In the early spring your crows will appear as reliably as the neighbor's dog trotting by the end of your driveway on his morning patrol, or the neighbor's cat crossing the foot of your garden on his daily mouse-hunting rounds. And because crows live for several years, the chances are that you will have the same crow neighbors for at least a few years at a time.

Sometimes even at this season you will see more than two crows some of the time. If you see three crows regularly, the chances are that the third bird is a helper. In a great many species of birds a nesting pair is assisted by an additional adult. In some species these helpers are very helpful indeed. They bring food to the young, chase off predators, and assist in the defense of the territory against potential competitors. Among crows the helpers seem to play a much more modest role. They may help the pair to defend their territory, and in return they are allowed to feed at peace in the territory. But when the breeding season begins in earnest, the helper bird is driven off by the resident pair. Now the number of birds you regularly see in your field will fall to two.

Some people regularly see *four* birds in their field in early spring. Four crows may feed in the same meadow if the meadow is large enough to accommodate two territories. The two pairs will have nest trees at the opposite ends of the meadow and they divvy up your meadow between them. Although crow neighbors are usually good to one another, you can sometimes see them skirmish over their boundary. The interaction is usually pretty subtle. You will see two of your four crows walking side by side across your field. You wouldn't think that there was anything special going on except for the fact that they are not feeding as they walk and except for the odd way in which they are walking. Their feathers may be all fluffed out, giving them a potbellied look and making their heads appear fuzzy. Their walk is very stiff and they waddle more than usual, as if the effort of keeping all those feathers fluffed out is making it difficult to walk. One or both crows may give the cawing display: they rock back and forth and appear by their motions to "pump" out a series of three or four caws.

Every once in a while you will see larger numbers of crows on your field in the spring. On these occasions there will be a lot of social action. The crows will fly restlessly about and caw loudly in many voices. They may even skirmish with one another. One will fly over to where another is perched, dive on it, and drive it away. The birds may wheel and twist in the air for a few seconds like fighter planes. What is happening is that a flock of nonbreeding crows is paying a visit to the territory of your regular pair. The visit is usually short-lived, and within an hour or so the flock has moved on and the number of crows feeding in your meadow has returned to two.

You might want to pay particular attention to these visits from flocks. Scientists are unsure how to interpret them. Everybody agrees that having a territory for a crow is like having a lease on a good apartment in a rent-controlled housing district. There appear to be many more crows around than territories to house them. But here the agreement ends. Some scientists believe that these visitors are relatives of the breeding crows who have stopped by to see how they are making out. Other scientists have a more sinister interpretation. They believe that these flocks of nonbreeding crows are trying to interfere with the breeding of the pair and are trying to get their territory away from them. If they find one of the territory owners missing or if the pair does not put up a stiff enough resistance to the invasion, then one or two of the flock birds will take over the territory.

Despite all these possible variations, you will probably have two crows in your field most of the early spring. Then suddenly, around the middle of April, you will notice that you see only *one* crow regularly. Also, the amount of crow noise you hear will suddenly diminish from a constant yammering to an eerie silence. You might suppose that one of your pair has been lost and that your territory is half-vacant. But in the crows' world an empty territory—even a half-empty one—is as impossible as an empty rent-controlled apartment in the city. Within hours, another crow from the nonbreeding flock lurking nearby would have taken over for a missing crow. Consequently, even though you see only one crow, it's almost certain that you still have your two crows living near your meadow. What's happened is that one of them, the female, is busy incubating eggs. While she sits on the nest the male either brings her food or watches over the nest while she feeds herself. Hence, during this period you see only one crow at a time.

Sometime in May you will begin to see two crows again. You will know then that the young have hatched out. As they grow larger and their feathers emerge, the young birds are able to control their own temperature and their mother no longer needs to keep them warm. Now both parents bend to the task of bringing food to the youngsters. All day long the number of crows in your field will shift from one to two to one as alternately the father and mother make the trip from your meadow to the nest. One moment both parents will be feeding in the meadow; then the father will take off and go to the nest; in a few minutes he will be back waddling beside his mate and pecking in the field. But then the mother will fly off to the nest, leaving the male alone in the meadow.

So far, your crow family have been very quiet neighbors. But as the young get larger they get noisier, until just before fledging—usually sometime in early June—when they become quite unruly. When they see a parent coming with food they make their plaintive bleating calls. Every time they are fed they make gobbling noises like soprano turkeys. When they leave the nest about five weeks after hatching, they are still poor flyers and they hide out in the trees around the nest, waiting for their parents to bring them food. If you listen carefully at this stage, you will hear the communication between the searching parents and the hiding young. First you will hear a parent's feeding call. It sounds a bit like a heron call or, come to think of it, a bit like a crow trying to caw with its mouth full. You can get the idea of it very nicely by trying to say "caw" with your mouth closed. It sounds something like "gock!" This call is uttered once every several seconds. The young respond with faint, wistful begging calls. The two sounds alternate until the parent finds one of the young and feeds it. You will know because you will hear the crescendo of begging calls and gobbling sounds that always occurs when a youngster is fed.

In a week or so the young become strong fliers and can get about on their own. At first they flounder around the tops of the trees near the nest. But one day, suddenly you will notice five or six crows in your meadow. These are the two parents and the three or four young from the nest. Although the young crows are nearly as large as their parents, they can be distinguished from the older birds because their feathers are less shiny and because they are relentless beggers. Every time a parent finds something to eat, the young will converge on it, hopping frantically, fluttering their wings, and calling as if death by starvation were imminent. Day after day the family will repeat this domestic scene in your meadow.

Beginning in late July or early August the numbers of crows in your meadow will begin to be more variable. Sometimes your crow family will be in residence and you will count five or six. Sometimes the young will be gone and you will count only the two parents. Sometimes a group will visit your meadow and you will see ten or twenty birds. What seems to be happening is that the young from neighboring territories are gathering in small flocks and moving about the area. These wandering flocks become larger and larger as summer proceeds into fall and they wander ever more widely. By autumn you may occasionally see large flocks, numbering as many as two hundred to three hundred crows. Now the local flocks are being augmented by migrating birds from farther north. As the snow line pushes southward it seems to sweep most of the crows with it. The young crows and the adult crows from the nonbreeding flock are the first to leave and they migrate the farthest south. The territory-holding older crows are the last to leave and will stay on all winter if they can manage to find a steady source of emergency food in the neighborhood—a farmer's silo, a piggery, a feedlot, or a not-so-fastidious town dump.

The number of crows in your meadow in deep winter will depend entirely on how far north you live. If you live in deep-snow country, your crows may disappear altogether for a few weeks or even a few months. They may have gone only a few miles to join a group living around a local food source; if so, your birds may return to your territory every few days to make sure that no competitors have gotten a hold. But your crows may also have migrated several hundred miles away. Every year gigantic groups of crows concentrate along the Eastern coastline and across the southern states from Maryland to Kansas. If you are host to one of these concentrations, you might have a *million* crows in your meadow.

A wintering group of crows is a remarkable social organization. The birds center their activities around a roost, a giant assembledge of birds that gathers each night at some traditional location, usually a grove of evergreens in an isolated location. Each day, the crows in the roost fan out in small parties, searching for food as far as forty or fifty miles from the roost. In the evening they collect again. If you live in the neighborhood of one of these roosts, you can see long lines of roost-bound crows in the late afternoon. Often these birds fly very high and they always fly directly, so that keeping an eye on the direction of late-afternoon flights of high-flying crows, you can triangulate the roost and figure out where it is.

The behavior of the birds at these roosts is remarkable. As each small party arrives, they dive toward the roost in great spirals. Each new group of arrivals seems to stir up the crows already there. Every so often the whole crowd takes off and swirls around the roost, cawing loudly. The birds are so numerous that from a great distance it may appear that the trees of the roost are on fire and eddies of smoke are rising over it. The noise made by such a large roost of crows is not only deafening but strange and uncanny as well. Not only are there the usual snarls and rattles of excited crows, but every imaginable kind of cawing sound can be heard as well. You'll hear slow caws and fast, long caws and short, high caws and low, cooing caws, whining caws, caws that are flat and caws that rise and fall in pitch. It is as if, in an effort to distinguish itself from every other crow, each crow improvises the most bizarre and unusual cawing pattern it can imagine.

As winter wanes, these huge roosts begin to break up. The migratory crows head northward and inland, leaving southern crows to defend their territories. In the North, the territorial pairs will return to their meadows and gradually the breeding season will resume.

Of all the familiar garden birds, the crow more than any other makes sounds that remind me of human speech. Compared to most birds, we human beings are grunters. We make lowish sorts of sounds. Most birds are peepers; they make high sorts of sounds. Crows appear to make sounds that are reminiscent of human grunting; they are grunters like us. The sounds sound lower because the crow modulates them. He causes the sounds to start and stop rapidly, and it is these rapid on/off alternations that our ears pick up, not the basic sound. Our ear interprets these alternations as continuous low-pitched sound. Because the crow's ear is faster than ours, it may be that the crow hears its own sounds not as continuous low-pitched sounds but as more or less rapid trains of clicks, similar to the rattling sounds we hear crows make at other times.

Another way in which crows' sounds are similar to our own is that they seem to have a primitive sort of grammar. Grammar is a set of rules governing how words are used and how they are put together to construct sentences. Because of grammar, we know that "to squash a plant" means something different from "to plant a squash," even though the words are the same. In a similar way, the basic sounds of a crow's language, its "caws," mean different things depending on how they are put together with other caws. The meaning is not only in the individual caw, but in the arrangement of caws as well.

The manner in which crows put meaning into and take meaning out of their caws is extraordinarily complicated. Sometimes different kinds of caws stand for different kinds of crowly "concerns." For instance, "aar" is used by babies to beg food, "cah!" is used by adults to warn of hawks overhead, and "grwowr" is used to warn of perched owls or cats on the ground. But if there are crows sitting in a tree side by side, and one is saying, "growr . . . growr . . . growr," the second, "cah! . . . cah! . . . cah! . . .," and the third "aar . . . aar . . . aar," then these caws have an entirely different meaning. Now each sound identifies the crow as an individual. To distant hearers, each crow is announcing, "I am a crow different from these two crows sitting next to me."

The way you can tell which meaning is intended by a particular sound is by listening to the arrangement of the caws. When a crow uses a particular sound to announce his individuality, he repeats the same sound over again in short bursts:

"Growr . . . growr . . . growr . . . . growr." Pause. "Growr . . . growr . growr . . ." Pause. "Growr-growr-growr." The repetition is very precise and the pace is very regular. By contrast, when a crow wants to use "growr" to talk about cats and owls, the sound will be made much more variably and there will be no regular pauses.

"GROWR growowr growr . . . grwow gr gr GRWOWOR rrowr growr" would surely tell you that the crow is worried about a cat or an owl. Similarly, "Aar . . . aar . . . .

AAAR .. aar ...... aar .. aaAAR .. aar .... aar" would
not be an individual crow using "aar" to identify himself,
but a baby crow calling to be fed. Finally, "Cah! .. caah ..
ca-uh .. ca ... ca-uh .... cah! .. cah .. CAH!" would warn
of a hawk circling overhead.

But the strangest kind of cawing of all occurs when
the crows mixes extremely different sounds together in
the same sequence. A crow that says, "Cah! ... cah! ...
car ... aaar aar .. raar .. graar .. growr ... growr ...
GROWRRR ... growrk .... cark! .. cah!" is "singing."
What singing means to a crow, nobody knows for sure.
But it means something different than it means to any
other bird. For most birds singing is used to proclaim a
territory or solicit a mate. But for crows singing seems
almost like babbling or talking to oneself. A singing crow
sits by himself, often in a sheltered or hidden spot away
from other crows. He makes sounds in the most
extraordinary sequences, as if he is playing and improvising with sound. He seems to get very excited about his
song. He may fluff up his feathers and arch his back. He
may peck vigorously at a leaf or a twig. Whatever the
song means, it seems to be of great emotional importance
to the singing crow.

The crow's language seems to have something to do
with his reputation for prodigious intelligence. Long
tradition, both in the United States and England, has it
that crows can count up to seven. I've talked to farmers on
both sides of the Atlantic and heard the same evidence. If
a hunter approaches a place where crows feed, sets up a
hunting blind, and goes inside, the crows are said to avoid
the blind until the hunter leaves it. If two hunters set up a
blind and only one leaves it, the crows will still avoid the
blind, apparently aware that there must still be a single
man inside. The same is said to be true of three hunters,
with two departing, of four hunters with three departing,
and so forth on up to seven. However, if eight hunters
occupy a blind, but seven leave, the crows are said to be

fooled and will come down to the ground to feed within range of the remaining hunter's gun.

I confess that I doubt the experiment was ever tried. Knowing what I know about country people, I just can't imagine eight sturdy hunters trooping into a blind together, nor can I imagine seven of them trooping away again without taking a shot. There's just too much dignity in country people for such foolishness—and too little time to waste on it.

But if crows do know how to count to seven, I think I know why. When a crow caws to identify himself, he gives the caws in bursts, each burst followed by a quiet period. On any particular occasion a cawing crow seems to pick a number of caws per burst and then sticks close to that number. Three is the most common number. A bird that is cawing three caws to a burst will sometimes caw four times or even five or two times or even once, but most of its caws will be in bursts of three. The number of caws in a burst varies from one up to seven but rarely beyond.

Now, I have always assumed that the number of caws in a burst is conveying some information, but I have never for the life of me been able to figure out what that information is. Once you write the sequences out in numbers they take on a numerological fascination. For instance, what did the bird have in mind that said, "3434343433434334?"

And what occurred in the world of the bird that said, "5555555553456777767?" to make him change from fives to sevens?

And, were two birds that were calling together and saying,

"2 2 2 3 3 3"
"3 3 3 3 4 4"

squabbling over who was to get to use threes? Whatever the meaning is, it seems clear to me that if crows make calls in numbers from one to seven, it might well be true that crows can count caws in numbers from one to seven. And if they can count caws up to seven, why not hunters as well?

The rain has eased up now, so I think I'll go back out in the garden to survey the storm damage. Fortunately, we were spared the worst of the rain and wind, and the garden looks refreshed, not beaten and drowned. Overhead the remaining clouds move stolidly toward the southeast. Just at sunset, their rear edge lifts clear of the western horizon and reveals the sun poised to set. The light slants under the edge of the cloud deck, making the eastern horizon suddenly an intense, deep blue. By contrast, every leaf in the garden sparkles with sunlit drops of golden water. The wet mesh of the chicken wire glistens.

As the sun dips below the hilltops, I catch a glimpse of a crow flying resolutely from the west field toward the watch tree. It is one of the parent crows, taking a last trip to the nest before the light fades and the rapacious babies begin their long nighttime fast. Under my breath, I wish the parent Godspeed and the babies good night. Such diligent parents deserve no less.

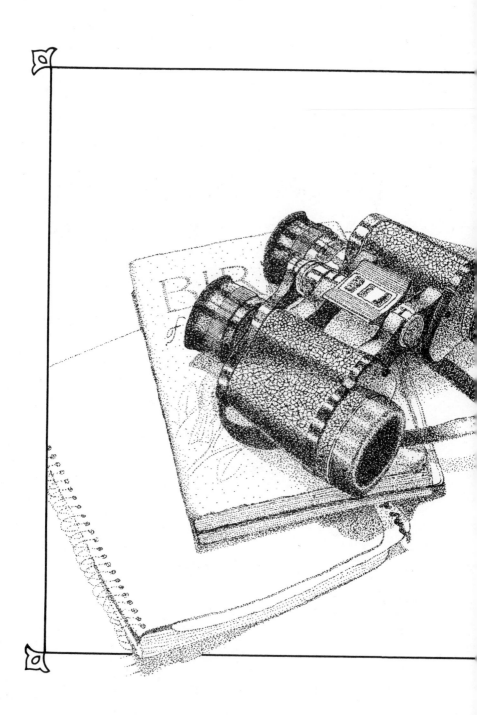

11
A Lifetime of Observing Birds

If I have been successful in my writing of this book, by now you may have experienced a new sort of relationship with some of the birds in your garden. You have felt the firm, dry grip of a chickadee's claws on your finger. You have shared with your robin his indignation at the intrusion of some mannerless robin trespasser. Perhaps you have compared and evaluated the song patterns of your song sparrow in the same way his neighbor or potential mates are doing. You may have watched with excitement as a party of house sparrows rushed through their frenetic mating display. Or maybe you have learned the bell calls of your local blue jays so well that you can tell as well as they can when a transient jay is in the neighborhood giving a foreign bell call.

What I hope is that these or similar experiences will spur you to a lifetime of enjoying the birds in your garden. In this last chapter I would like to give you some information about things that you can do, books you can read, and equipment you can purchase to help you continue to learn about your bird neighbors long after you have finished reading this book. But first of all, I would like to clear away some of the mythology about what it means to be a bird watcher.

Briefly, my message is that there are bird watchers and then there are Bird Watchers. Every one of us knows, by reputation if not by direct acquaintance, at least one avid Bird Watcher. These individuals are rather awe-inspiring. They are up at dawn and off to the woods toting telescopes, tripods, and cameras. Their yards are outfitted with birdhouses of every architectural style, their hedgerows planted with a bewildering array of fruiting shrubs. In winter they set up myriad feeders of intricate design that provide a gourmet smorgasbord of seed, fruit, and fat to please the palate of the most discriminating of wintering birds. Bird Watchers often travel in groups and use obscure Latin names, which they eagerly tick off on printed sheets of paper known (somewhat ominously) as "Life Lists." Such individuals as these set a very high standard indeed for what it means to observe and enjoy birds.

If, as a consequence of reading this book or as a consequence of other experiences, you have determined to become a Bird Watcher, then this last chapter may seem like weak fare for you. In that case, feel no need to linger here. There is a world of books and gadgets and organizations eager to lead you to the highest levels of Bird Watching expertise. Fortunately, public library collections of bird watching literature are as voluminous as on any subject, save perhaps weight reduction. The countryside abounds with bird lovers' organizations that sponsor field trips, workshops, and night school courses. Call your local evening school program, go to your public library, write your local chapter of the Audubon Society. Your possibilities are unlimited, and there's no time like the present to begin.

But you do not have to be a Bird Watcher to get a great deal of pleasure from watching birds. I would like to dedicate this chapter to readers who anticipate a more private, more casual, more incidental program of observing birds. I think particularly of gardeners. Gardeners are people who are outdoors a lot but whose thoughts are often taken up with weighty matters: When to Plant, What to Plant, Where to Plant It, and all the other myriad concerns that a gardener carries about as he or she perambulates the garden. I hope that such readers, while you probably do not want to make a serious hobby of bird watching, still will want to augment your pleasure in the garden by increasing your knowledge of and your contact with the birds that inhabit it.

This chapter, then, is devoted to helping you with just such an easygoing program of bird observation and appreciation. All you really need for a lifetime of casual bird study are good eyes, good ears, and an immense amount of patience. But in addition, it is helpful to have a garden with lots of variety, some nesting boxes, a good pair of binoculars, a few good books, and a bird feeder.

A Garden with Lots of Variety

The first step in your bird appreciation program is to begin to think about your garden the way gardeners in England think of a garden. For Americans, the garden is a plot within a larger piece of property referred to as a yard. To an English gardener, the garden is not simply a plot in which to grow flowers and vegetables, but an environment for the house and its inhabitants. The English gardener practices horticulture avidly from one boundary of his or her property to the other.

The key to having a rich variety of bird life—or life of any sort, for that matter—in your garden is understanding the principle of the ecological niche. The ecological niche is the role or place that each organism occupies in nature. A bird's niche is the sum of all the physical requirements that the bird has and all the ways in which it interacts with other species. If a bird needs to bathe in water or in dust, then the water or dust in your garden is a part of its ecological niche. If a bird provides food for hawks or cats, then hawks and cats are part of its ecological niche. If a species of bird needs a nesting cavity to raise its young, then holes in old apple trees are part of its ecological niche, and so also are the other species of bird that compete for the use of such holes.

Each species of bird has its own ecological niche. What this means is that no one kind of food, or nesting site, or hiding place, or foraging site, or bathing location is likely to satisfy every kind of bird. It also means that the more variety you have in your garden, the more species of birds you are likely to have living there. Consequently, when you are thinking about attracting birds to your garden, you want to think about not only what birds need—food, water, cover, and nest sites—you want to think about how you can fulfill these needs in as many different ways as possible.

From a bird's point of view, the ideal garden has a variety of "provinces." Some areas have short grass that is kept well mowed and well watered, while other places have high grass that is allowed to go to seed. Somewhere in such a garden are found tall trees that cast deep shadows and provide food and nesting sites for the species of birds that live in treetops. Elsewhere in the bird lover's garden are bushy thickets or dense evergreens where some birds feed and where many others seek shelter from wind, storms, and night-prowling predators. Instead of having only one kind of fruiting shrub, such a garden has several different kinds that will come into fruit at different times of the year. Instead of a single stone birdbath, it offers a variety of different ways in which birds can get to water. There is probably a place where the water stands in a pool, and another place where it trickles, and yet another place where the ground stays wet and mucky most of the summer.

If you are an organic gardener, you will be glad to know that you have already taken many steps that will have the effect of increasing the diversity of bird species in your garden. A well-managed organic vegetable or flower garden has a rich and varied soil life that provides luxurious feeding opportunities for many kinds of birds. Moreover, the absence of any pesticides in the garden means that the birds can feed there safely, without the risk of getting a dose of chlorinated hydrocarbon along with their meal of cabbage loopers or earthworms.

A Bird in the Bush
Is Worth Two in the Hand!

You are striding across your lawn, pushing your mower, when all of a sudden you notice something fluttering in the deep grass ahead of you. A butterfly? A felled bird? You stop the mower and tiptoe cautiously over to have a look. There in the grass is an object that looks like a bird—only uglier. Its color is all mottled and its wings look ragged. It is a baby bird, a fledgling of a few hours—or worse, a nestling, fallen from the nest. What do you do?

Nothing! Or almost nothing. The young of many species of bird leave the nest before they are able to fly well. The babies disperse in the trees near the nest, and the parents continue to feed them assiduously. Parent and offspring locate each other through a system of special calls. Mostly the babies sit still and wait for the parents to come to them, but if the parents are reluctant to approach them, the babies may try to fly to the parents. The fact that you have found this baby on the ground has something to do with the fact that you are mowing. The mowing disturbed the parent birds enough so that they wouldn't approach the baby. The baby tried to make the flight and did not quite succeed.

Why not bring the baby inside and raise it yourself? There are four good reasons: (1) it is illegal; (2) the chances

Nesting Boxes

Your pleasure in having birds in your garden will be increased if you put up a few nesting boxes. Attracting birds to nesting boxes requires no special expertise. Any roughly appropriate structure will attract the interest of several species of birds within minutes after you set it out. What makes birdhouses the subject of so much technical argument is the problem of attracting particular species of are slim that you will hit on the right mixture of food before the baby starves to death; (3) it will require feeding a couple times an hour, all day from dawn to dusk (are you sure you have the time?); and (4) even if you do succeed in raising it to the age that it can fly well, the chances that the baby bird will live to reach a happy adulthood are negligible. The fledgling period is an important period of training for the young birds, one in which they learn from their parents what they should eat and what dangers they should look out for. Male fledglings even learn something about how to sing. Even with all their natural training, young birds have a terrible time making it through their first year. Do you really, honestly think your ignorant, hand-raised baby could survive?

The best thing to do is leave the baby alone. As soon as you go away, the parents will begin to feed the young bird in the grass. In a few minutes it will regain its strength enough to make its way into the lower branches of a shrub. At the very most, pick the young bird up carefully, cupping it in your hands to restrain it and put it up high, out of harm's way: on a twig, in a nest, on the roof of a shed, anywhere where it will not get stepped on or snatched by the cat. Then take yourself and your mower to another part of the yard for an hour or so. The parent birds will take care of the rest.

birds while not attracting others. Here also, the basic principle of variety applies. The more your nesting boxes vary in design and placement, the more different kinds of birds you'll be likely to attract. Put a box with a small entry on a long pole out in an open area not too far from water, and you may get tree swallows. Make the entry smaller and dangle the box from a limb of a large tree, and house wrens may move in. Give the box a larger entrance and put it on a fence post next to a small sheltered pasture or orchard, and you might attract bluebirds. Each design and location will favor one species over another.

The simplest way to provide nesting boxes for some of your birds is to go down to your local hardware store, buy a few, and try them out. If you get a bird you like, leave the box where it is. If you get a bird you do not like, try another location. Remember to attach the house to its support in such a way that you can take it down again. You can use screws, or double-headed nails, or some sort of mounting bracket, just so long as you can take the house down and move it if you are not happy with the clientele you attract. And don't get discouraged. Every birdhouse operator I know houses a few starlings and English sparrows from time to time, despite the best of efforts.

One or More Bird Feeders

As with getting birds to live in the nesting boxes you provide, there is no problem with attracting birds to a feeding site. Although bird food mixes are sold with great fanfare and at high cost in supermarkets and hardware stores, the fact is that birds of most common wintering species will come eagerly for mixtures of sunflower seed with cracked corn, millet, or peanut hearts. These items can be purchased inexpensively in bulk at feed stores, and you can store them in a garbage can to keep them dry and safe from rodents. Even the choice of a feeder itself is no problem. Most birds are content to take seed off the ground, or off a porch rail or off the roof of an outbuilding. Just be careful not to leave heaps of seed out in the rain; it gets moldy. Either shelter it or scatter it. And beware of creating a bird trap by scattering seed where your cat has a good hiding place. Pick a place where your feeding bird guests will have good sight lines in every direction for several feet.

The complexity of bird-feeding arrangements arises from trying to feed some species to the exclusion of others. Obviously, if you do not want to feed squirrels and you live in a wooded area, you are going to have to resort to a special feeder of some sort; and if you are troubled by flocks of ground-feeding birds, you may want to use a feeder that requires the diner to perch rather than walk. Such a feeder will favor birds with strong feet, such as chickadees and nuthatches. If you want to favor small birds over large ones, consider an enclosed feeder with an entrance hole or a feeder with a weight-sensitive perch that closes the feeder when a heavy bird lands on it. As with birdhouses, variety among feeders is helpful. The more different foods and the more different kinds of feeding sites you make available, the more kinds of birds you are likely to attract.

Still, the point is not to let all these complex decisions interfere with getting started on your feeding program. Any feeding arrangement and any seed mix that includes sunflower seeds will get you on your way. Once you have a regular clientele coming to your backyard, you can improve on it if you like by making special arrangements or serving special foods.

A Pair of Binoculars

The joy of having a good pair of binoculars is that it is so easy to watch birds without disturbing them. The same opportunities for bird watching can often be realized by sitting quietly in the garden for several minutes, but most of us lack that kind of patience. The binoculars make it possible to see the birds up close without waiting for them to come to us. There are dozens of different kinds of binoculars. Try a pair outside before you buy them. As you are trying them out you should be thinking about quality, power, aperture, width of field, and portability.

167

Essentially, a pair of binoculars is two small telescopes set in a rigid frame that keeps both at the same focal length and pointed at the same subject. Binoculars are good or bad depending on the sturdiness of the frame and the quality of the lenses. Sloppily constructed binoculars can be worse than none at all. Looking through binoculars that are slightly out of kilter can make you feel cross-eyed in a few seconds and give you a severe headache in a few minutes. What happens is that the two eyepieces of a poorly constructed pair of binoculars present to the eyes different images, which they vainly struggle to fuse. Since the difference between good and bad binoculars is often subtle and difficult to discern from a quick inspection, the only solution is to buy the binoculars from people you really trust, who stand behind what they sell. I used to buy bargain binoculars at discount houses. But after getting real junk (in nice leather cases) a couple of times, I now get my binoculars only at my local camera shop. I pay a bit more, but I do not get stuck.

Printed on the frame of most binoculars you will find a formula, such as "7 × 35." The first number of the formula is the power of the binoculars, the amount that they magnify the image. You would think that the magnification of a pair of binoculars would be its most important feature and that binoculars would vary tremendously in their degree of magnification, but most are either seven- or eight-power. For backyard birding, seven- or eight-power is sufficient, and the difference between them is so small that you are free to make your decision on other criteria. The other crucial number listed on the binoculars is the aperture, the size of the large lenses opposite the eyepieces. These are given in millimeters and are usually 25 mm, 35 mm, or 50 mm. The size of these lenses determines the light-gathering properties of the binoculars. If you expect to use your binoculars under dim light conditions, then the larger lenses will be helpful to you.

But remember: the larger the lenses, the larger must be the metal frame that holds them, and therefore, the larger the binoculars overall. For most purposes, apertures of 25 mm or 35 mm are entirely adequate.

Also imprinted on the binoculars is a number that represents their width of field, usually something like 350 feet at 1,000 yards. Wide-angle binoculars let you look at more landscape at a single glance, and some have widths of field as great as 750 feet at 1,000 yards.

Binoculars also vary tremendously in size and weight. Some birders are fond of miniature binoculars that can be tucked inconspicuously into the small pocket of a jacket. Despite their relative convenience, however, these miniature binoculars are too delicate and fidgety for the taste of other birders. Other things being equal— particularly quality—miniature binoculars will always be more expensive. If you like the convenience and are willing to pay the money, then these miniature binoculars may be just the thing for you. But I would be careful not to sacrifice quality in order to get portability. Such a sacrifice would be a bad bargain indeed.

Nobody can tell you what kind of binoculars are best for you. For what it is worth, you might consider the following recommendation. In recent years I have purchased Bushnell 7×35 binoculars with the Instafocus feature, a device that slightly increases the convenience of focusing the binoculars. They are large enough and sturdy enough to let me see easily, yet small enough to fit comfortably into the outside pocket of a windbreaker. They are widely available, and I recently purchased a pair at my local camera shop for under $60.

A Few Good Bird Books

In recent years several excellent field guides have been published. Three of which I am particularly fond are the new edition of the Peterson *Field Guide to the Birds*

169

East of the Rockies (Boston: Houghton Mifflin, 1980); its companion, *Field Guide to Western Birds* (Boston: Houghton Mifflin, 1972); and *The Birds of North America* (New York: Golden Press, 1966). These are durable, pocket-sized paperback books. They have lavish color illustrations arranged to facilitate comparisons among similar species. Both provide range maps that reveal at a glance whether any particular bird is likely to be found in your region.

The differences between the "Peterson" and the "Golden" field guides are subtle but might be important to some readers. The Peterson text gives more detailed information about each species and the color illustrations seem just a bit fresher and more lifelike. On the other hand, the Peterson presents its range maps in a separate section at the back of the book, so to find all the information on a single bird you have to look it up twice. Also, remember that the Peterson covers only North America east or west of the Rockies. If you travel to the other side of the Rockies, you will have to buy the other book. The *Field Guide to Western Birds* is available only in an older edition.

Similarly, the Golden field guide has both advantages and disadvantages. One of its advantages is that it includes all the North American birds. Wherever you go in Canada, Mexico, or the United States, the Golden guide is still useful. Also, its range maps are right next to the illustrations, so that you have all the information about each bird available at a glance.

When experts identify a bird, they are as likely to use its sounds as they are its plumage pictures. Both guides present verbal descriptions of the sounds of each bird. But the Golden supplements its visual descriptions of many birds' songs with voiceprints. Simply put, a voiceprint (or sound spectrogram) represents a song in the form that is analogous to musical notation. As in musical notation, up and down indicates higher and lower pitch and left to right indicates time. A quick glance at a voiceprint tells you something about the cadence of a song and about the quality of its notes. Thin horizontal lines on the sound spectrogram indicate simple pure tones, many parallel lines stacked one on top of another indicate rich tones, and a wide smear indicates a noisy sound. The Peterson does not have voiceprints, but its verbal descriptions are usually fuller. In addition, the publishers will sell you a record (contact Houghton Mifflin Co., Wayside Road, Burlington, MA 01803) that is keyed to the pages of the field guide, so that you can flip pages and listen to the birdsong simultaneously.

If you are more a gardener than a bird watcher, you may have tried to use a field guide in the past and been discouraged. Despite their deceptively colorful and decorative appearance, field guides are not all that easy to use. There is a fundamental problem: to identify a bird you have to locate its picture in the book among the hundreds of other pictures. Without a pretty good idea of the bird's identity, such a search is a frustrating task. So it would seem that field guides divide all the world into two sorts of people: those who know enough to use a field guide but don't need one, and those who need a field guide but don't know enough to be able to use it. So how could field guides be of use to anyone?

The fact is that you have to get to know a field guide gradually. The more you familiarize yourself with it, the more useful you will find it. It is not a book to be read like a novel, nor is it a book you turn to only when you are looking for a bird. It is a book you rummage around in whenever you have a free moment. The best way to get to know a field guide is to start by reading the entries on the birds that are old friends to you. Look closely at their pictures and notice how they do (and how they do not) resemble the birds you know. Most field guide illustrations are slightly schematized to emphasize each bird's distinguishing characteristics. By comparison with the drawing, the real bird in front of you will often seem a bit imperfect. The colors will often not seem quite so crisp as they do in the book, the feathers never quite so evenly arranged. Remember, too, that each bird, like every person, is an individual. Each bird you see in the garden may have slightly different markings than the picture of the bird in the book. On the other hand, sometimes subtle differences are all that distinguish between two entirely different species. As you page through your guide, you will gradually develop a feel for what differences are crucial (they are called field marks) and what differences may be safely disregarded.

As you have read the entry for one of your familiar birds, read the other entries on the same page. These will usually concern species of birds that are closely related to the bird you started with. Read the descriptions carefully, trying to get a sense of what the birds of a group share in common and what characteristics differentiate them. If the text mentions other birds that are not closely related but still are similar in plumage or behavior, look up those and study them as well.

Once you have done some reading in your field guide, you will be in a position to use it to identify some birds. Whenever you see a bird that you do not recognize, ask yourself which of the birds that you do recognize most resembles it. Turn to that part of the book and flip pages back and forth, looking at the illustrations. Chances are you will see your bird after a few seconds of hunting.

Other Useful Reference Books

Donald W. Stokes has recently written a new kind of field guide, *A Guide to the Behavior of Common Birds* (Boston: Little, Brown, 1979). Stokes's book features detailed descriptions of the yearly cycles and day-to-day habits of twenty-five of the most common birds. Some of the prominent behavior patterns are illustrated with delightful marginal drawings. The presentations are not as well integrated as I would like, but on the whole it is a delightful and useful book for those who want to study what birds' behavior means and how it fits into the birds' life cycles.

The best field guide to birdsong was written by F. Schuyler Mathews at the turn of the century, *Field Book of Wild Birds and Their Music* (New York: Putnam, 1910). Mathews saw birds as musicians. He presents each song as a musical composition, extolling refinements in tempo and harmony with all the reverence and enthusiasm of a musicologist at a symphony concert. The Mathews book is long out of print, but fortunately it was widely purchased by libraries, many of which have it still. For gardeners with a musical bent, this book is an absolute must.

But my favorites of all bird books are a series of volumes compiled by Arthur Cleveland Bent, *Life Histories of North American [species name]*. Each volume assembles what was known in the 1930s and 1940s about the members of a large taxonomic group of birds. For instance, one volume is devoted to North American cardinals, grosbeaks, buntings, towhees, finches, parrots, and "allies"; another to "crows, jays, and titmice," and so forth. Not only do these works contain every fact you could want to know about the birds described, but they often contain fascinating quotations from original field notes describing particularly remarkable or curious occurrences in bird life. The writing is very skillful, even elegant in places. Despite their age, these books are still available as reprints in bookstores with particularly good natural history collections.

Finally, you might want to own one of the numerous books that have been written on the subject of attracting

173

birds to the garden. Almost any library, no matter how small, will have at least one, perhaps several titles on this subject. One that I like particularly is George A. Harrison's *The Backyard Bird Watcher* (New York: Simon & Shuster, 1979). The book is particularly thorough and well illustrated, and it gives easy-to-follow, detailed guidelines for feeding, housing, and planting for birds.

Gardeners Make the Best Bird Watchers

While I have spent this last chapter describing books and gadgets that will help you with your bird watching, still I want to stress that all you really need for a lifetime of bird study are sharp eyes, keen ears, and a lot of patience. Of all people interested in birds, gardeners perhaps have the least need for bird-watching accoutrements. Because you are frequently attending to your garden, your birds have come to take you into their confidence. As long as you move slowly and continue about your regular gardening chores, they will provide you with many opportunities to observe the most intimate details of their lives.

It is important to take these opportunities when they are offered. They often come at the worst of times—when you are rushing to harvest the peas, or snatching a few moments of early-spring twilight to get in your first crop of beans and spinach, or scurrying to get in a late crop of beans in July. Then the sparrow will come and perch on the pea vines a few inches from your head, or the crow will pick a fight with an owl in the evergreens across the pasture. Or the robin will wrestle a giant worm to the surface a few feet down the row from where you are working. These moments of intimacy with your birds are as much the fruit of your gardening efforts as the fresh peas or corn or greens you eat. Harvest them gladly. Stop what you are doing for a moment, shift yourself slowly and carefully into a posture you can hold for several minutes, and take the time to watch and listen to your birds.

These are occasions that will imprint on your memory, in a way that no book can ever do, the typical sounds and field marks of a bird. This is the time to study the details of the plumage, to invent for yourself a mnemonic device to identify the bird's sounds. If you take these opportunities willingly whenever they are offered, you will come to know your birds in a way no expert ever can teach you.